Labour and the Unions

Other discussion pamphlets in this series sponsored by the Campaign Group:

Andrew Glyn   *A Million Jobs a Year: the Case for Planning Full Employment*

Ben Lowe   *Peace through Non-alignment: the Case for British Withdrawal from NATO*

Labour and the Unions

A discussion pamphlet sponsored by the
Campaign Group of Labour MPs

———◆———

JOHN KELLY

VERSO

London · New York

First published by Verso 1987
© 1987 John Kelly

Verso
UK: 6 Meard Street, London W1V 3HR
USA: 29 West 35th Street, New York, NY 10001 2291

Verso is the imprint of New Left Books

British Library Cataloguing in Publication Data

Kelly, John E.
  Labour and the unions: a discussion
  pamphlet sponsored by the Campaign Group
  of Labour M.P.s.
  1. Labour Party — Great Britain
  2. Wage-price policy — Great Britain
  3. Trade-unions — Great Britain —
  Political activity
  I. Title   II. Labour Party *(Great Britain).*
  Campaign Group
  339.5'0941   HC260.W24

ISBN 0-86091-894-7

Typeset by Photosetting, Yeovil, Somerset
Printed and bound by CPI Group (UK) Ltd, Croydon, CR0 4YY

Contents

Acknowledgements

I would like to acknowledge many helpful comments on earlier drafts of this pamphlet by members of the Campaign Group and the Socialist Society.
   Details of books or articles cited in the text will be found in the reference section at the end.

Foreword

This booklet has been produced at a most opportune time.

- For eight years the unions have been under attack from a succession of Conservative governments. This attack has included legislation to reduce the effectiveness of trade unionism and to diminish individual employment rights, the mobilization of the police to deter picketing and demonstrations in major industrial disputes, the cutting of social security benefits for dependents of striking workers, the abolition or curtailment of various protective measures for low-paid workers, women and youth, and a sustained campaign by government spokesmen, aided by the greater part of the media, to denigrate trade unionism in the eyes of the public.

- The return of mass unemployment and the decline of the traditional industries, in which there is a high density of trade union organization, has confronted the movement with new problems.

- In the 1987 General Election campaign, many of the Tory attacks on trade unionism went virtually unanswered. In almost every interview given by Mrs Thatcher, scathing comments were directed against trade unionism. The failure of the Labour Party to respond adequately to these was not, in my view, an accident or an oversight. The indications were that it was the result of a decision taken within the Labour leadership to 'soft peddle' on trade unionism and not to give a prominent public place to leading trade unionists.

In such a political environment, I commend this booklet for three main reasons. Firstly, it challenges the view that the unions are now so weak that they have to adapt themselves to a 'new realism', implying a retreat on many issues. John Kelly, the author of this booklet, acknowledges that the trade union movement has suffered defeats during Mrs Thatcher's period of government and that the new laws have introduced substantial difficulties, but

1

he also points to evidence of the continuing strength and vitality of trade unionism. The loss of membership has not been as proportionately heavy as during previous periods of industrial depression. Pay increases have been negotiated for millions of workers at least equal to the rise in the cost of living. At the workplace level, the unions have maintained intact their organizational roots and in some areas have even extended them. In the political fund ballots the unions were successful to an extent which very few, friend or foe alike, anticipated.

It is necessary to emphasize these positive points as an answer to those who argue that the days when the trade unions – and the organized workers in general – formed the bedrock of the labour movement have gone for good. I have never found this cry of pessimism persuasive, whether it comes from the right, the centre or from contributors to *Marxism Today*. It is based on a false and outdated analysis of what constitutes the working class and demonstrates a failure to recognize the continuing vital importance of the struggle for workers' interests, whether in the traditional industries or among, for example, white collar technicians employed in the micro-electronics industry.

Secondly, this booklet helps to explain why so many trade unionists did not support the Labour Party in the 1979, 1983 and 1987 general elections. It was not that working people had somehow lost their concern about defending and improving living standards. On the contrary, many felt disillusioned in 1978 and 1979 when a Labour government, despite the advances made in earlier years, sought to hold down the pay of some groups of workers below the rise in the cost of living. This was the price to be paid for the government's other failings in economic policy. To many citizens it was an unacceptable price. The memory of the 'winter of discontent' still casts its shadow over Labour's fortunes.

In 1983, the Conservative Party received a lower percentage of votes than in 1979, but Labour lost even more substantially. The damaging split in the Party – not only the formal split represented by the formation of the SDP, but the attacks on Party policy from within the Party during the election campaign – came not from the left but from the right wing, from some of the very people responsible for the disillusioning policies of the earlier years.

In 1987 the Conservative Party polled about the same proportion of the votes cast as in 1983. Labour started the campaign well behind, and the evidence suggests that there was no likelihood that the Tories would be overtaken in the three or four weeks before polling day. Indeed, according to the public opinion polls, it seems that Labour *lost* support during the election campaign itself. At the beginning of the campaign, Labour, the public was being told, had the support of between 31 per cent and 35 per cent of the electorate. Some commentators even placed Labour's probable support at between 35 per cent and 38 per cent, based on polling evidence from local elections, and Mr Kinnock himself was confidently predicting victory. In the event Labour polled less than 31 per cent of the total vote with, as everyone now knows, a marked disproportionate movement of votes in the regions.

Why, in national terms, did Labour lose support during the election campaign or, at best, fail to make progress? This time, unlike 1983, there had been no significant splits in the Party just before the election, nor attacks on the Party's policy during the campaign from preceding Labour Prime Ministers and no fever generated by military victory in the Falklands.

Some of the reasons for the outcome of the 1987 General Election are, of course, outside the scope of this booklet or of this foreword. But some of the reasons do have a bearing on trade unionism and the economic interests of working people.

The gains in Labour's vote in Scotland, Wales and the north of England underlined the importance of economic issues in determining voters' preferences. The electorate in these regions was very much aware of unemployment and industrial decline. The very good results in Liverpool – despite the almost universal denunciation of the local Labour council by the Tories, the Alliance, the media and the Labour leadership – demonstrated the positive effect of a policy of popular struggle around such issues as housing and local employment. Mr Eric Heffer, for example, who is not of the Militant Tendency but who defended the Liverpool Labour Party's record on housing, local government finance and other aspects of policy, increased his parliamentary majority by no less than 9,000 votes, representing a swing to Labour of 11.2 per cent. The issues were well known to the electorate, and Eric Heffer's role in defending the record of the Liverpool Labour Party had assumed national prominence. He lost his seat in the Shadow Cabinet, lost his seat on the National Executive Committee of the Party and identified himself sharply in opposition to Neil Kinnock's attacks on the Liverpool Council. The election results in Liverpool, and particularly the heavy swing to Eric Heffer, cannot be disregarded by any serious commentator on the labour movement.

There is no permanent gain for Labour, even in the more prosperous areas, when it distances itself from trade union struggles against the consequences of a reactionary government and bad employers. Nor is Labour likely to evoke enthusiasm among employed workers, particularly skilled and higher paid workers, when they are told, on the one hand, that a Labour Government would increase the basic rate of tax but, on the other, that any savings from nuclear disarmament would be used not for health care and education but for

3

increased conventional arms spending. Incidentally, the 1986 annual conference of the Labour Party, in one of its resolutions on defence policy carried by a large majority, called upon the Party 'to stress the need for a planned transfer of public spending from weapons to welfare and industrial development . . . ' This was not put forward in Labour's election campaign.

The third reason why I commend this booklet is that it strikes a radical, realistically optimistic note, not only in its analysis but in the remedies which it advocates. Labour needs radical policies on jobs, living standards, the social services and the organization of the economy. These policies need to be radical because of the depth and intensity of the problems now facing Britain. They will not be formulated in consensus with the representatives of big business. They must be designed to reduce the power and influence of big business. Policies which present a clear alternative in terms relevant to the everyday interests of working people are likely to be electorally more successful.

With the election of yet another Conservative majority in the House of Commons, even though only a minority of the electorate voted for it, new attacks are likely to be launched against trade unions. The broad outline was sketched in a government paper, 'Trade Unions and their Members', published in February, 1987.

Legal encouragement will be given to strike breakers even when a majority of workers concerned have voted for strike action. Unions will be denied any disciplinary means of ensuring that majority decisions are observed. Legal changes will make it easier for dissidents to prevent the democratic control of union funds. The ultimate weapon may be to use a device invented by the courts during the mining dispute: to remove the control of a union from its elected representatives and instead to place it under a 'receiver' appointed by a court. State control of 'trade unionism' would thus be sanctioned by law. Further impediments are likely to be instituted against union membership agreements or arrangements and further state interference is likely in the procedures of unions for choosing their representatives. Finally, a new inquisitor may be created by law, to be known as a Commissioner for Trade Union Affairs. The effect will be to encourage and assist dissidents who object to the implementation of decisions reached through the representative machinery of the union.

These possible, indeed probable, new attacks will stimulate counter-action. Trade unionism will continue to assert itself because it is needed by workers in their everyday life. On issues such as jobs, security, employment rights, participation, a shorter working week and an earlier minimum retiring age, the struggle will not be abandoned. It will continue. Similarly, the government's proposal to end the rating system and to introduce a so-called

4

community charge, under which most working people will pay more and the rich will pay less, will have its repercussions on industrial relations. Put simply, many workers are likely to fight back and to seek to protect themselves, among other means, by claims for higher pay.

The way forward is not to fudge the issues, not to replace specific radical measures with rhetoric, not to speak of consensus when what is required is the prosecution of the interests of the majority against an exploiting minority, and not to create the public impression that the left is an embarrassment to Labour. Such attempts to move the labour movement to the right may win encouraging sounds from newspapers which oppose Labour but they are unlikely to gain electoral support. The result will not be to win support for Labour but to strengthen the anti-Labour prejudices of some working people who do not feel the immediate threat of unemployment, whose living standards may have risen and who have reasonable housing conditions. The question they are likely to ask is that if Labour's leaders are embarrassed by trade union struggles and if Labour's leaders are seen to be concerned about the so-called 'loony left', why should they – the more prosperous among working people – give the Labour Party their electoral support? Thus the attacks on the left from within the labour movement, on the grounds that the left are an embarrassment, become self-fulfilling.

Neither I nor other sympathetic readers of this booklet are likely to agree with every observation made by the author. The responsibility for the views expressed remains exclusively with him. His views deserve attention and, in my view, the main thrust of his arguments are good and helpful.

Jim Mortimer
June 1987

Introduction

In the past twenty years two Labour governments have suffered electoral defeat in the aftermath of a wave of strikes organized and led by the trade unions. In both cases government-union relations had deteriorated as Labour's policies, in office, drifted to the right and workers bore the costs of the government's attempts to restructure British capitalism. The damage that has resulted from splits between the industrial and political wings of the labour movement has made the relationship between them into a central political question. On this relationship could hang the fate of the Labour Party, in or out of government. It is therefore imperative that socialists should scrupulously and critically examine its future contours.

In the aftermath of the 1987 General Election there will be widespread concern in the labour movement to maintain and improve the relationship between the Labour Party and the trade unions. Labour leaders have too often regarded the unions merely as a vital source of funds and have preferred not to give them an active and central role in campaigns. Indeed, Labour leaders have almost invariably offered only lukewarm support for industrial struggles, such as the miners' strike, and have been half-hearted in their opposition to the Tories' anti-union legislation. And in the run-up to the 1987 General Election, John Edmonds felt it necessary to criticize Labour's leaders for the way in which they had kept the unions out of the campaign.

At the same time, the Labour Party has been anxious to secure union agreement to its programme, not least because it will almost certainly entail some form of incomes policy. Yet this agreement has been reached for the most part in closed committee rooms, and it is doubtful whether Labour's policies on industrial relations and the economy are widely understood, or supported, by rank and file trade unionists. The 1987 Election Campaign was widely acclaimed and many of Labour's social policies undoubtedly serve the interests of millions of ordinary people. Yet the fact remains that in 1987, 54 per cent of trade unionists voted Tory or Alliance, and just 43 per cent voted Labour. And whilst Labour did well amongst semi-skilled workers (46 per

6

cent voted Labour) and the unemployed (52 per cent Labour), it attracted just 35 per cent of skilled manual workers, compared to 42 per cent who voted Tory (Kellner, 1987). One of the central questions raised by these results is whether Labour really concerned itself sufficiently with the economic interests of organized workers.

Trade unions must obviously pursue a broad range of social and political issues, but first and foremost they exist to protect and improve the terms and conditions of employment of their members. And just as organized workers look to their trade unions to improve pay and conditions, so trade unions look to the Labour Party to advance the economic situation of working people as a whole. Labour's representation in local and national government enables it to improve terms and conditions of employment and workers' rights, and encourage the spread of trade union membership, and its policies in these areas will be considered later in this pamphlet. But even its most progressive policies have formed elements of a total package in which considerable sections of the working class are asked to accept pay restraint. If Labour is to defeat the Conservatives at the next election it must therefore seriously re-appraise a set of policies which many organized and skilled workers in 1987 apparently found unacceptable. It is these policies, above all for industrial relations and trade unions, which this pamphlet sets out to examine.

Prior to the election, the TUC-Labour Party Liaison Committee produced a series of documents describing a set of rights to be enacted for workers and trade unions, a set of proposals for reducing low pay, and ideas on the increased involvement of trade unions in economic policy-making and technical change. Labour also promised to reduce unemployment by one million in two years. In return for such measures reached through a 'National Economic Assessment', a Labour government would be looking to the unions for some form of wage restraint. In other words Labour offered something like a new 'Social Contract', with some form of incomes policy, despite occasional and mild protests to the contrary. Regrettably, Labour's plans were, in this respect, within reach of the policies advocated by the Alliance.

Labour and TUC documents dropped very clear hints on these matters for those who care to read them. According to *Partners in Rebuilding Britain* (1983) a Labour government would pursue a clear order of priorities: first putting the unemployed back to work; second, improving the living standards of the low paid; and third, improving living standards for the rest of the population (1983, para.20; see also *A New Partnership, a New Britain*, 1986, p.18). The implication was that some ways would be found for restraining the pay demands of the third group, and this implication emerged in accounts of the National Economic Assessment, a tripartite forum at which union and

7

party leaders and employers would discuss a range of economic indicators with a view to reaching agreement.

According to Neil Kinnock, 'In the National Economic Assessment, therefore, government, management and trades unions must strive to achieve agreement on investment and income, on costs of production and consumption, on incomes and on prices; for they are all part of the same whole. It is, of course, a revenues and rewards policy' (Kinnock, 1986, p.160; see also *Partners in Rebuilding Britain*, 1983, para.18; *Low Pay*, 1986, para.96). And a similar account of the National Economic Assessment has been reiterated in the most recent Liaison Committee document, *Work to Win* (1987, pp.11–12).

In other words, the clear statements about priorities and the scope of the National Economic Assessment both point in the direction of an incomes policy. That nobody uses the phrase 'incomes policy' is neither here nor there; it is the substance of the policies that is important, not their labels.

The question for socialists is whether incomes policies and the like would be in the interests of the working class as a whole, and whether, in the words of a previous manifesto, they would shift the balance of wealth and power towards working people and their families. The answer to that question depends on the answers given to three others. First, what is the present state of the trade union movement? The impact of recession on the trade unions will significantly influence both their willingness and their ability to cooperate with government and to push for more radical measures. Secondly, what lessons have been learned from the previous Social Contract of 1974–79? And thirdly, what would be the impact of Labour's measures on the rights and interests of workers and trade unions?

The central argument of this pamphlet is that despite eight years of recession trade unions still retain considerable bargaining power. They would therefore be reluctant to repeat the experience of the Social Contract, when living standards fell. Nor would they be persuaded to co-operate in wage restraint for any sustained period by Labour's new legal measures and related policies. These would significantly improve the protection of trade union organization, and the terms and conditions of employment of millions of low paid and mostly unorganized workers. But they would offer much less to organized workers whilst insisting they bore the brunt of pay restraint. If Labour is to become the voice of the vast majority of the working class it must pursue more radical policies that will unite rather than divide workers. Let us therefore consider in turn, the state of the trade unions, the 1974–79 Social Contract, and Labour's proposals, before finally considering how socialists ought to respond.

1

The State of the Unions

One reason for thinking that trade unions *will* be willing to create close relations with Labour, accept a greater role for the law in industrial relations, and cooperate in economic and technical change, derives from the view that they have become chronically weak in recession. According to this view, trade unions have suffered so badly in recent years that they have reached a watershed in their history: the massive loss of members, the effects of unemployment and anti-union legislation, the defeats suffered by major groups of workers (notably miners and printers), the disastrous election results of 1983 and 1987 and the swing to the right in public opinion not least among trade unionists: all these factors are thought to signify a major turning point in the history of trade unionism. The old methods of industrial militancy and free collective bargaining, it is argued, are less and less effective, and what is said to be required is fresh thinking, and a willingness to reconsider policies that were previously taboo: a statutory national minimum wage is one example, a legal right to a pre-strike ballot is another, incomes policy is a third (see for example, Carter, 1986; Coates & Topham, 1986; Hain, 1986; Hobsbawm, 1985; Rowthorn & Grahl, 1986; Sherman, 1986). Are the unions actually in such a state of crisis? And if so, do we need to rethink union policies along the lines mapped out by the TUC-Labour Party Liaison Committee documents?

That trade unions in Britain today face a series of immense problems and difficulties is beyond dispute and it would be foolish and complacent to minimise them. But it is equally wrong to exaggerate them or to see them out of context. Let us look in turn then at trade union membership and organization, working conditions, strikes, wages, employers and the state and public opinion.

(a) Trade Union Membership

Between 1979 and 1985 TUC membership fell from 12.2 millions to 9.5 millions, a decline of 22 per cent (TUC *Congress Reports*). Total trade union membership (TUC and non-TUC) fell during the same period from 13.5 millions to 11.0 millions, a drop of 18.5 per cent (*DE Gazette*). Trade union membership *did* occasionally fall in the postwar period (1949–50, 1953, 1958–9, 1962, 1966–7, 1971), but the losses were small, sporadic and quickly made up particularly between 1968 and 1979. The recent loss of membership has been unevenly spread as the following table shows:

Trade Union Membership Changes 1979–1985

TGWU	−31%	NALGO	−0.1%
AUEW/AEU	−26%	NUPE	−4%
GMWU/GMBATU	−15%[1]	EETPU	−13%
ASTMS	−21%	USDAW	−18%

1. This figure is relatively low because of the merger between the GMWU and the Boilermakers Union in 1983. If the merger is discounted, the GMWU would have lost 25% of its membership between 1979 and 1985.

Source: *TUC Statistical Statements* 1980, 1987.

Concern has also been expressed about the financial health of trade unions, particularly in the light of widespread redundancies amongst employees of the AEU, announced in early February 1987. In general though, trade union finances have weathered the recession reasonably well, and very few unions have reported expenditures in excess of income. Three types of union have experienced financial difficulties in particular years: firstly, those who have organized large, long strikes, viz., NALGO (1979), NUT (1980, 1985), NGA (1980), ISTC (1980), CPSA (1981), POEU (1983), NUM (1985); secondly, craft unions which still pay considerable sums of unemployment benefit, viz., AUEW/AEU (1981, 1984), NGA (1981), ASB (1982); thirdly, unions which

10

failed to increase membership subscriptions quickly enough to offset a rapid loss of members and/or a rapid rise in costs viz., UCATT (1978, 1980), SCPS (1980), ASTMS (1981), CPSA (1982), NUPE (1985), AEU (1985), (see Kelly, in press). Unions that have faced chronic and persistent financial problems, such as the printers or the engineers, are the exception rather than the rule.

But how *serious* is the overall loss of membership? One yardstick is to compare it with membership loss in previous recessions that have followed sustained periods of union growth (the pattern from 1968 to 1987). We find that between 1890 and 1893 the trade unions lost almost 40 per cent of their membership, and between 1920 and 1923 they lost 35 per cent (Cronin, 1979, Table B.10). In the three years 1979–1982, trade unions lost 14 per cent of their members, a considerably smaller loss than in previous comparable three-year periods.

More detailed evidence shows that the bulk of this recent membership loss occurred in private manufacturing because of the closure of large, organized plants. Membership in private services and the public sector has hardly changed at all (and may even have increased a little). Furthermore, the proportion of workplaces where pay is negotiated through collective bargaining has risen between 1980 and 1984 from 55 per cent to 62 per cent (Millward & Stevens, 1986, p.226), despite a fall in union density (the proportion of those in work who belong to a trade union) from 57 per cent (1979) to 51 per cent (1985).

(b) Union Organization, Working Conditions and Strikes

The closed shop has been the most obvious victim of Tory legislation, with the number of workers covered by closed shop arrangements falling by over a million between 1980 and 1984 (Millward & Stevens, 1986, p.107). On the other hand, the number of shop stewards and full-time lay representatives has remained unchanged over the same period, with a rise in the number of public sector stewards offsetting their predictable decline in manufacturing (Millward & Stevens, 1986, p.84).

If we turn our attention to workers and their conditions of employment, we have witnessed a massive rise in unemployment to approximately 3.75 millions; extensive reorganisation of working practices and increased effort levels in many parts of industry and the public sector; and the privatization of parts of the health service and local government, with a consequent deterioration in conditions of work.

Finally, there has been a dramatic decline in the number of strikes: in the

11

1970s the annual strike frequency never once fell below 2,000; in the 1980s it has never once been *above* 2,000 and has twice fallen below 1,000.

Some commentators have been particularly struck by these findings, and have seen in recession the seeds of a 'new industrial relations', epitomised most clearly by the practices of the EETPU. For a number of years that union has pioneered an approach to employers consisting of several elements: strong support for productivity improvements through flexibility and the ending of job demarcations; single union agreements to end inter-union squabbles; no-strike agreements and pendulum arbitration to avoid interruptions to production. In return the union has pressed for reasonable wage settlements and limited measures of worker participation in decision-making (see Bassett, 1986). Other commentators have discerned the emergence of a two-tier labour market based around 'the flexible firm' with a core of skilled, well-paid, secure workers at the centre, and a periphery of insecure part-timers, temporary contract workers and homeworkers (Atkinson & Gregory, 1986).

How extensive are these practices? And what effects will they have on trade union organization? Some of them have been exaggerated out of all proportion: the so-called 'no-strike' deals probably cover no more than about 20,000 workers, less than 0.4 per cent of the British manufacturing workforce, and are unlikely to spread because of union resistance and employer uncertainty (Sherman, 1986). Their main effect is likely to be an ideological contribution to that section of public opinion hostile to strikes. Other measures, such as single-union agreements, may actually benefit workers by reducing the incidence of sectional disputes over jobs and membership (though they can be damaging if introduced without consultation and agreement).

It is certainly the case that part-time working has increased in recession, and that few part-time workers belong to trade unions. But in areas of strong union organization such as the NHS or local government, it has proved possible to organize considerable numbers of part-timers, suggesting they are not as resistant to trade unionism as is sometimes thought (Bain & Price, 1983, pp.24–5).

It is probably the case that 'flexibility' and 'productivity agreements' have spread through industry since 1978, and that in many firms working practices have been altered, particularly with the introduction of new technology. Whilst these changes have almost certainly been associated with job loss, especially in manufacturing industry, and have probably contributed to rises in labour productivity, there is no evidence that they have damaged union organization. In any case it is a mistake to assume that the break-up of 'restrictive practices' or worker controls based on job demarcations necessarily diminishes workers' power at the point of production. New systems of labour flexibility often require extensive cooperation from workers in moving from job to job, and if conditions permit, this cooperation can be withheld from the employer and used as a power resource in bargaining to extract concessions.

Finally, so far as strikes are concerned, all previous evidence suggests that the strike pattern is strongly cyclical: strike frequency rises during economic booms, peaks on the threshold of recession, declines as recession bites and unemployment rises, only to rise again with economic recovery and the growth of trade union membership. This has been the pattern as far back as 1888 and there are no grounds for thinking it is about to change, and that strikes are a thing of the past.

(c) Wages

One of the most striking features of the recession has been the growth of real wages for many of those in work. The average earnings index for the whole economy (according to *DE Gazette* figures) remained equal to or above the Retail Price Index throughout 1978, and then dipped several percentage points below the RPI in the second half of 1979. From late 1979 until the middle of 1981 average earnings increases generally exceeded the rate of inflation. The latter half of 1981 witnessed price rises overtaking the growth in average earnings, but for the next four years (1982–86) average earnings rose faster than prices.

According to Rowthorn and Grahl (1986), 'real wages for those fortunate enough to keep their jobs have risen much faster in the UK since 1979 than in any other major western country' (1986, p.26). Manufacturing earnings have risen in real terms by 18 per cent between 1979 and early 1986.

If we take the earnings figures for the whole economy then on *average* workers in recession have not done too badly on the pay front, suffering real pay cuts only in 1979 and 1981, but experiencing real pay rises between 1982 and 1986.

If we break down these figures into different economic sectors then a rather more complicated picture starts to emerge. In general, the average annual earnings rise in manufacturing industry has exceeded those in the public sector services, where government has been largely successful in holding down pay rises at and often below the rate of inflation. (The above figures have been taken from various issues of the *DE Gazette*). As a result many of the most bitter strikes of the 1980s have been fought by public sector employees over

13

wages – steel, coal, water, civil service, health service, education. In addition, many groups of poorly-organized, low-paid workers in the private sector have fared badly as Wages Councils have been abolished, the Fair Wages Resolution scrapped, and other legal rights removed. Increasingly, then, the working class has divided in its experience of recession.

The fact that many groups of employees have secured real pay rises during several years of recession is not in itself proof of the efficacy and vitality of trade unionism. Employers have sometimes had their own reasons for wanting to boost pay, such as the need to attract and retain skilled labour that is often in short supply. And with the recovery of profits from 1983 many have been able to afford pay rises at or above the rate of inflation. But it is significant that *union* criteria for pay rises – increases in the cost of living, and comparisons with other groups of workers – are still widely cited by employers even in the depths of recession, suggesting that so far as wages are concerned and especially in manufacturing industry, union power may not have fallen as much as people sometimes think (Gregory et al, 1985; Millward & Stevens, 1986, pp.246–7).

It is true that very few people actually *feel* their standard of living is rising (Goodhart, 1985, Tables 2.9, 2.10). Nevertheless the available evidence suggests that those in work have fared better, on average, than in the years of the Social Contract (1974–79) when earnings simply kept pace with inflation, but did not exceed it (Glyn & Harrison, 1980, p.117). And it is also worth noting that a similar rise in living standards was experienced by many of those in work in the 1930s Depression.

(d) Employers and the State

But what about the attacks on trade unionism by employers and the State? Surely union organization must have suffered at their hands since 1979? It is certainly the case that the number of strikes has declined since 1979, and that 'secondary' industrial action is now very rare because of the draconian fines meted out to the NGA in the *Stockport Messenger* dispute. Indeed employers do seem more willing to go to the courts for injunctions to prevent secondary action or to force unions to hold a pre-strike ballot. And particular examples of overt 'union bashing' or confrontation with unions are not hard to find – MacGregor at the Coal Board and Murdoch at Wapping are the most recent and prominent cases. But we must go beyond particular cases and situations and ask just how widespread and systematic has the 'employers' offensive' been?

14

Overt attacks on trade union organization and facilities, and dramatic restrictions on the scope of collective bargaining have been concentrated in three types of firm: parts of the State trading sector and public sector services, where we have witnessed major confrontations in every year of Thatcher's two governments as tight controls on public spending have been enforced and labour 'shaken out': BL (1979), British Steel (1980), Civil Service (1981), NHS (1982), British Rail (1982–83), Water Boards (1982), coal mining (1981, 1984–85), teachers (1985–86) and the newly-privatized British Telecom (1987). Secondly, a minority of private manufacturers who have been especially hard hit by recession and seen their market share eroded by more efficient competitors have also tried to restrict union rights and unilaterally alter working practices (Batstone, 1984). Thirdly, in some low-paying firms in the services sector there has been growing contempt for Wages Council orders and a rise in the number of firms failing to comply with their wage rates.

The other side of the coin is that in most sectors of manufacturing and in parts of the public sector, such as some local authorities, employers have not pursued strategies of overt confrontation. They have continued their existing bargaining and consultative arrangements with trade unions and have preferred to introduce change through negotiation rather than unilateral imposition (Millward & Stevens, 1986, pp.64–9). They have also been willing to reach pay settlements above the rate of inflation, partly because profits are booming, and also to attract skilled workers who are now in short supply in key areas of work (electronics engineering) or in certain parts of the country (the South East). For their part unions have largely cooperated in restructuring and rationalization. Some unions felt they had no choice because of their firm's weak competitive position; others have cooperated in such change over many years and were not therefore being asked to do anything radically new in recession; consequently many employers have faced a fairly cooperative trade union movement and have therefore had no incentive to launch an offensive against shop stewards or collective bargaining. This is not to say that unions have been docile in respect of changes to work practices, but only to say that the resistance they have offered has rarely been so effective or on such a large scale as to force the employer into a wholesale attack on union organization.

(e) Trade Unions and Public Opinion

The final aspect of unions to be addressed is their popularity and standing in the opinion polls. That the Thatcher government has attempted to weaken trade unions and blacken their image is clear enough, but how successful has it been? It is not easy to measure the public standing of trade unions, but one source of data is the Gallup answers to the question whether unions are 'a good or a bad thing'. Responses to this annual poll show that approximately two-thirds of the adult population regard unions as 'a good thing', a figure which has been remarkably stable since the first such poll in 1954. Large strikes or strike waves can depress union popularity, as in 1972 (55 per cent said unions were a good thing), 1974 (54 per cent), 1975 (51 per cent), 1977 (53 per cent) and 1979 (51 per cent). It may be that, paradoxically, the decline of strikes under the Thatcher government has displaced unions from the public consciousness, and since 1981 their popularity (measured by the Gallup polls) has risen to its highest level for twenty-two years (Gallup Political Index, 1985, 1986; Fogarty, 1986, p.88).

This is not to say that strikes always reduce the popularity of unions, still less that they benefit the Conservatives, the employers or anti-union governments. Since 1979 there has been a succession of disputes which for a time weakened support for the Conservative government, and aroused public sympathy for the workers directly involved: health workers in 1982, the denial of trade union rights to GCHQ workers, the harsh treatment of striking miners in 1984–5, Murdoch's confrontation with printworkers at Wapping in 1985–6, and the occupation of the Caterpillar works in Scotland.

These and other events often failed to transform public sympathy into union solidarity, but they probably helped unions to chalk up a resounding success in the political fund ballots. Between 1985 and 1986 all 38 unions with political funds voted overwhelmingly to retain them, by majorities of about 5:1 on an average turnout of 62 per cent. Moreover four unions have since voted to establish political funds for the first time, and NALGO will shortly ballot its members on setting up a political fund (*Labour Research*, May 1986; October 1986).

Taken as a whole the evidence on public opinion about trades unions does not confirm the existence of any simple and major drift to the right. But nor does it suggest that all the talk of attitude change in response to 'Thatcherism' can be dismissed as so much hot air. Public opinion is both complex and contradictory, providing positive focal points for the Left to work on, as well as obstacles to overcome.

*

In general therefore, and with some notable exceptions, unions have weathered the recession remarkably well. Membership and density have declined, but less than in previous recessions; workplace organization has remained largely intact and is still expanding in the public sector; real wages for many of those in work have increased since 1981; and unions were completely successful in the political fund ballots.

Some readers however will regard these conclusions as inaccurate, optimistic and complacent. Surely, it will be said, the recession has done immense damage to workers and trade unions, a fact that is evident in the sufferings of the miners, the collapse of manufacturing in the North of England, the intensification of clerical work in the DHSS offices and so on. How can we square these facts with the claim that some unions and some workers have weathered the recession reasonably well? And even if the trade union movement has come through the recession in reasonable shape, aren't economic and occupational trends running against trade unionism? The decline of large manufacturing plants, the growth of the service sector and part-time employment, and the expansion of well-paid white collar workers: all these trends must surely augur badly for a trade union movement based in manufacturing and the public sector?

There are four points to bear in mind. Firstly many of those in work have paid for their increased earnings with higher productivity: British manufacturers now produce 5 per cent more than in 1980 with 25 per cent fewer workers. Secondly, the costs of restructuring and recession have been unevenly spread: a core of better-paid, professional, managerial and skilled workers has done reasonably well since 1981, particularly in the South East, whilst a large periphery, made up of the unemployed, other benefit claimants, low paid service workers (mainly women), young people and certain ethnic minorities, have done very badly (Leys, 1985, Table 2). Thirdly, the behaviour of most employers in the current recession is remarkably similar to the picture that emerges from the Depression of the 1930s. 'In general, employers' associations took little fundamental advantage of union weakness. Individual employers were often ready – at least until the beginnings of revival after the mid-1930s – to practice workplace encroachments upon standard terms and conditions, but there were no collective aspirations among them to overthrow union regulation altogether' (Fox, 1985, p.357).

Of course, trade unions do face an inhospitable climate because of government policies, employer practices and changes in working class composition and outlooks. But it should not be assumed that these problems are novel or insuperable, or that unions will not respond. Trade unions have previously seen their membership decline or stagnate in the face of restructuring and the rise of new groups of 'anti-union' workers. Irish immigrants, semi-skilled workers, clerks, women, managers, scientists, technicians: in the past all these groups posed a challenge to the imagination and resources of the trade union movement, but after initial difficulties, unions have succeeded in gaining substantial membership amongst all these sections of workers. There is no reason to assume that what has been done in the past cannot be achieved in the future. The recruitment drives amongst low paid service workers by the TGWU and GMB, and the merger between TASS and ASTMS to create one of Europe's largest white collar unions, are two strategies which indicate union responsiveness to change, and alternatives to the business unionism of the EETPU. It is worth noting that the unions which have pursued 'no strike', 'single union' deals with employers have not thereby successfully staved off a decline in membership. Preliminary returns for 1986 show that the EETPU and AEU lost 130,000 members compared with the previous year: this is a rate of decline about double that of the average for TUC affiliated unions. Fortunately business unionism is not the majority response to the challenges the unions face.

*

In conclusion then, trade unions and their members have come through this recession surprisingly well, despite the many difficulties and pitfalls they have had to face. Above all, workplace organization and collective bargaining have remained largely intact as employers on the whole have not embarked on an anti-union rampage. On the other hand unorganized workers in low paying industries and parts of the public sector have almost certainly suffered real cuts in living standards and remain vulnerable to the power of the employer.

The working class experience of recession is therefore uneven, divided between the well-organized and relatively powerful core groups and the low paid and unorganized periphery.

What is the *political* significance of this assessment? For all the reasons given earlier – the (historically) modest decline in union membership and density, the survival of workplace organization, and the persistence of collective bargaining – the resources of the trade union movement remain considerable. This *ought* to be a source of strength for a future Labour government and it shows that such a government will have to pay very close regard to the views of the trade union movement.

2

The 1974–79 Social Contract

The experience of 1974–79 provides the nearest model to the type of arrangements likely to emerge under a new Labour government, and it is therefore instructive to consider just what was achieved in this period, and why the Social Contract collapsed.

There are those in the movement who look back on the Social Contract years with some fondness. Union leaders had privileged access to the corridors and committee rooms of power; union-party relations were better than they had been for many years; and the main planks of Labour's programme, in office, enjoyed the support of the trade unions who had indeed helped to create them. But the honeymoon was brief and following intervention by the IMF in 1976, the government's economic policy drifted to the right as it pressed ahead with the battle against inflation, despite a growth in unemployment and at the price of public sector spending cuts and wage restraint.

What then, did the Social Contract set out to achieve? Its main goals were described in the document, *Economic Policy and the Cost of Living* (TUC, 1973), and included the following: a commitment to full employment, the improvement of living standards, a more equitable distribution of income, increased welfare spending, industrial restructuring and modernization, and the regulation of inflation through price controls.

(a) The Achievements ...

So what were the achievements of the Social Contract and what lessons does it hold for the future? Firstly, trade unions and their members obtained a number of legal rights as part of a package of measures strikingly similar to those currently on offer. The previous Conservative legislation (the Industrial Relations Act, 1971) was repealed although its sections giving protection against unfair dismissal were largely re-enacted. In addition, trade union immunities (freedom from civil action in the courts) were restored and extended, closed shops were given greater protection, and union representatives were allowed paid time off work for certain trade union duties and training. ACAS was created, primarily for conciliation and arbitration purposes. It also had powers to conduct inquiries into and adjudicate upon recognition disputes; unions had the right to receive certain types of information from their employer, and to be consulted over redundancies; health and safety representatives were to be elected, and to have some limited powers in all workplaces. In addition, there was a Committee of Inquiry on Industrial Democracy which finally produced the Bullock Report. And, on paper, Labour was committed to a much more interventionist industrial policy orchestrated through the Department of Trade and Industry and the National Enterprise Board via the mechanism of planning agreements. It is important to bear these points in mind, because as we shall see, on paper Labour's new programme is remarkably similar to that of the 1974 government, though weaker in analysis and commitment.

Many of the legal measures did take effect: there was a substantial growth in the numbers of workers claiming redress for unfair dismissal, and in the numbers of shop stewards attending both general and specialist training courses; an additional 1.5 million workers were brought under closed shop agreements; health and safety representatives were quickly established in many workplaces; and the voluntary conciliation service of ACAS enjoyed trade union support. In addition the Equal Pay Act finally came to fruition and many low paid workers benefitted both from this measure and from the £6 a week increase under the flat-rate incomes policy which operated in 1975. Labour also produced a White Paper on Industrial Democracy which was a watered-down version of the Bullock Report's recommendations for worker directors on the boards of large companies. A number of union leaders (Jack Jones and Clive Jenkins for example) were strong supporters of the Bullock proposals, but there were equally passionate and convinced opponents. Frank Chapple (EETPU) and Hugh Scanlon (AUEW) were, for different reasons, in favour of extended collective bargaining but against worker directors, whilst the GMWU's David Basnett expressed serious reservations about the proposals. Just as significant as these divisions was the lack of interest amongst many rank-and-file unionists, a stance that contrasted dramatically with the CBI's militant opposition to Bullock. Caught between a powerful, united and intransigent employers' organization, and a disunited and uninterested trade union movement, the government backed away from the Bullock proposals.

Secondly, inflation was reduced from 25 per cent per annum in 1974 to 11 per cent by 1979. Thirdly, manufacturing output recovered from its 1975 slump, though by 1979 it was still below the pre-oil crisis 1973 peak (Prest & Coppock, 1982, p.194). Fourthly, trade union membership rose by 1.7 millions in those five years and in 1979 reached an all-time high of 13.5 millions (12.2 millions in the TUC) with 57 per cent of the employed workforce in unions.

(b) . . . and the Costs

What is striking about this period is that despite the early, close relations between union and party leaderships and the successful enactment of a wide range of legal rights, the trade union movement was finally driven to abandon its commitment to incomes policy because of the government's abandonment of the movement's economic and social policies. Behind the trade union decision lay a number of critical *economic* trends. First, unemployment rose from approximately 600,000 in 1974 to 1.3 millions in 1979, peaking en route at 1.4 millions in winter 1977. Secondly, living standards, even for those in work, fell between 1975 and 1977 more than at any other time in post-war Britain (Glyn & Harrison, 1980, pp.117, 118). Thirdly, by 1976 Labour had abandoned its interventionist industrial policy and expansionist economic policy and had begun to curb public spending.

Labour's ditching of its more radical plans and perspectives was followed and re-inforced by the formation of the Lib-Lab pact. This further set the scene for confrontation with its own supporters. Indeed Callaghan has explained in his memoirs that he was moved to respond to Liberal overtures by the prospect of a Labour back-bench revolt against the economic policy of his government (cf James Callaghan, *Sunday Times*, April 12, 1987).

Though it is well known that the Social Contract broke down in a wave of strikes during 'the winter of discontent', it is important to be clear about exactly *which* workers took industrial action to break the incomes policy norms and why. Four major groups can be identified: firstly, there were workers whose customary differentials had been squeezed (whether by incomes policy or by changed bargaining arrangements) e.g. BL toolroom workers (1977) and Heathrow baggage handlers (1977). Secondly, there were well-organized groups in profitable firms or industries who resented the growth of profits whilst wages were being restrained, e.g. Ford workers (1978) and road haulage drivers (1978–79). Thirdly, there were public sector workers with long standing pay grievances and anomalies who were no longer prepared to wait for their correction and chose industrial action, e.g. firefighters (1977). And finally there were public sector workers who had simply got left behind in pay bargaining as they had for a number of years accepted settlements inferior to those in the private sector, e.g. hospital ancillaries (1979), local authority manual workers (1979).

In conclusion, then, it can be seen that although Labour successfully extended worker and trade union rights in the 1970s, these (and other measures of social policy) were not sufficient to sustain the Social Contract for more than three years. The policy disintegrated amidst intense and widespread discontent over pay that was backed up by industrial action. It was cuts in living standards and the growth of unemployment that fuelled workers' discontent with Labour's performance in office, a discontent that was exacerbated by Labour's refusal to adopt any of the macro-economic measures supported by the TUC and which ultimately led to Labour's defeat in 1979. So what are the prospects for a new Social Contract?

3

Labour and the Unions: the new proposals

The TUC-Labour Party Liaison Committee (a body with representatives from the TUC General Council, the Labour Party NEC and the Parliamentary Labour Party) has now sketched out the broad outlines of Labour's industrial, economic and industrial relations policies, particularly in so far as they affect the trade unions. Broadly speaking Labour proposed to reflate the economy by an increase in public expenditure and borrowing of £6 billion, which would be divided between special employment measures (such as youth training, or community programmes), selected infra-structure projects (such as replacement of the sewage system, or housebuilding) and increased expenditure in existing areas such as health and education. In manufacturing industry Labour aims to encourage investment and modernization and to insist that unions play a full role in the drafting and implementation of such policies. "A new partnership" between labour, capital and the state is envisaged. The primary benefits accruing to unions and their members would be (i) the reduction in unemployment and increased economic growth, and (ii) a series of individual and collective rights designed to secure union and worker cooperation with Labour government policy and their acceptance of industrial modernization. Most of these rights are set out in two documents, *People at Work: New Rights and Responsibilities* (1986) and *Low Pay: Policies and Priorities* (1986) though some have been referred to or elaborated in earlier documents as far back as 1982.

(a) Individual Employment Rights

People at Work (PAW) proposes the extension or creation of rights in the following areas:

(i) *Unfair dismissal*   More workers would be given protection against unfair dismissal (such as part-time and new workers) and the normal remedy for an unfairly dismissed worker will be reinstatement (PAW, para.41).

(ii) *Part-time and temporary workers*   They would be given full legal rights in the field of employment protection regardless of their hours of work (PAW, paras.42–3).

(iii) *Statutory National Minimum Wage*   This would be phased in and set at an agreed level, with annual indexation to earnings. It would be policed both by trade unions (where they exist) and by a new Minimum Wages Inspectorate with powers of prosecution. Complaints might be taken either to the Inspectorate or to the Central Arbitration Committee whose awards would be legally binding. It is stressed that *both* union organization *and* statute law would be essential in the drive against low pay (PAW, para.46; *Low Pay* (LP)).

(iv) *Training programmes*   These would be extended and improved and there would be more facilities for paid educational leave from work (PAW, para.41).

(v) *Equal opportunities*   These would be improved both by changes to existing legislation and through the mechanism of contract compliance. In other words government and local authority contractors would be required to observe minimum equal opportunities standards and policies. There would also be more rights to paternity and maternity leave (PAW, para.45).

(vi) *Union ballots*   A statutory framework would lay down 'general principles for inclusion in union rule books based on a right for union members to have a secret ballot on decisions relating to strikes, and for the method of election of union executives to be based on a system of secret ballots.' (PAW, para.70).

What impact would these measures have on workers' terms and conditions of employment? The first three proposals (unfair dismissal, part-timers' rights and a national minimum wage) would almost certainly benefit substantial numbers of workers. In 1985 there were approximately 40,000 cases of unfair dismissal heard in the industrial tribunals (ACAS, 1986). In 1984 part-time workers comprised 21.4 per cent of the workforce in Great Britain, about 4.4 million people, almost 90 per cent of whom were women (Labour Research Department, 1986, Table 1). Most of these workers were employed in shops, schools, health services, hotels and catering establishments and miscellaneous services. The number of low-paid workers will clearly vary with the precise definition of the term that is employed (see Pond, 1983), but the Liaison Committee document set an initial target minimum wage of £80 per week (or £2 per hour), a policy that in 1985 would have benefited 3 million workers, two thirds of whom worked part-time. The modesty of this proposal becomes apparent when it is compared with earlier statements from the TUC and the Low Pay Unit. Pond (1983) for instance, recommended a minimum wage of £85 per week in 1982.

Of the other proposals, the training measures are so vague that it is quite impossible to judge their effects. In the field of equal opportunities contract compliance has been shown by the GLC to be a potentially very powerful weapon and is likely to make some impact on the rights of women workers, particularly in unorganized or weakly organized firms.

Finally, the union ballot proposals essentially re-enact Parts One and Two of the Trade Union Act (1984). In *general* they are unlikely to have a widespread impact because so many union rule books already met the Act's criteria in 1984 or have since been changed to do so. (Undy & Martin, 1984, p.59). Nevertheless the possibility remains that particular unions, e.g. NALGO, TASS, COHSE would find themselves in conflict with the courts if Labour pursued these measures.

For the Labour leadership, and for some union leaders as well, the right of workers to insist on a strike ballot must be enshrined in law. They either see this right as just one of a comprehensive package of rights at work (as is the case with GMBATU) or they see it as a responsibility that unions must carry in order to balance the rights they will obtain in other areas, such as recognition, or picketing (Wilson, 1986).

Socialists have four fundamental objections to these ballot proposals. The first is based on the belief that trade unions are and must remain wholly independent of the state. It is unions and their members, through the union's own procedures, who must decide how a union shall run its affairs and reach decisions. Secondly, the available evidence suggests that trade unions have revised and amended their procedures over the years to enhance their accountability to their members. NUPE and NALGO adopted systems of shop steward representation in the early 1970s. NUS and the AUEW introduced secret postal ballots for executive elections at the same time. CPSA voted in 1980 to elect its officials instead of appointing them. USDAW and many other unions set up working parties from the late 1970s to improve the representation of women within their organizations. Other unions, such as IRSF and SCPS, have commissioned outside researchers to examine their overall structures. Recent evidence shows therefore that in general unions have been willing to examine their structures and change them accordingly. Thirdly, socialists object to the interference of the courts in trade union affairs because of the well-known and overwhelming hostility of the judiciary to trade unions and collectivist values. And finally, in those few cases where the ballot proposals would have any effect, it would almost certainly hinder the union's effectiveness by delaying strike action. With 'perishable' issues such as victimization, or a change in working conditions imposed unilaterally by the employer such delay could prove very damaging.

What about the *costs* for workers of achieving the improvements promised by Labour in the areas of employment protection and minimum pay? These gains would not be costless because some firms might find it hard to pay the additional wage costs imposed on them, whilst others might be reluctant to hire part-time employees if their rights were to be made commensurate with full-time employees. Whilst it is difficult to quantify the effects of legislation whose details are not yet fully worked out, it appears that the introduction of a national minimum wage might affect youth employment, but would have much less effect on female part-time employment (Pond & Winyard, 1983).

In general therefore it is reasonable to conclude that several million low paid, part-time and female workers *would* benefit from Labour's proposals to extend individual employment rights.

If this is correct (and some would argue it is an optimistic scenario) what impact would it have on Labour government-trade union relations? What little information we have suggests that the majority of those who would benefit from these measures are currently not trade union members. According to Dickens at al. (1985), in the most comprehensive research to date on unfair dismissal, 68 per cent of tribunal applicants do not belong to trade unions. There is little reliable data on part-time workers in unions, though a recent survey of women workers found that whilst 49 per cent of full-timers did not belong to unions, the figure rose to 72 per cent for part-timers (Roberts & Martin, 1985). Figures for the industrial sectors that employ large numbers of part-timers show a similar picture. In retail distribution, there are approximately 850,000 female part-timers and of the *total* workforce in the retail sector 85 per cent were *not* trade union members in 1979 (Labour Research Department, 1986, Table 2; Bain & Price, 1983, Table 1.5). In miscellaneous services, another large area of part-time employment, 92.7 per cent of workers did not belong to trade unions in 1979 (Bain & Price, 1983,

Table 1.5). On the other hand in education, health and the entertainments industry, part-time workers are quite highly organized, though good figures are not available. Since the population of low paid workers largely overlaps with that of part-timers, much of what has been said about the latter also applies to the former. In other words the probability is that most of them do not belong to trade unions.

Now it is true that several major unions (TGWU, GMBATU for example) have recently launched recruitment drives targeted at part-time workers. It is also the case that the spread of legal rights could encourage many more workers to join unions. Nevertheless, for the forseeable future trade unions will continue to be dominated by full-time workers, and it is their views and interests that will predominate in union policy-making.

In conclusion, then, the main point to establish about Labour's programme of individual employment rights is that it would benefit several million workers, many of whom are women, but most of whom are not trade union members, and the significance of this point will become clear shortly.

(b) Collective Rights

The main collective rights proposed by the Liaison Committee are as follows:

(i) *Health and safety* Higher penalties for health and safety violations, compulsory provision of more occupational health facilities and increased powers for Health and Safety reps (PAW, para.47).

(ii) *Union recognition and organization* This would be facilitated by the provision of new recognition rights coupled with new statutory minimum standards of trade union facilities (PAW, para.50).

(iii) *Redundancy* Employers would be obliged to give earlier notice, to discuss trade union counterproposals and to pay higher levels of compensation (PAW, para.38).

(iv) *Industrial action* Restoration of union immunities, coupled with clarification of the law on picketing, and prohibition of some types of injunction against industrial action. In addition workers would have a right to have secret ballots on strike decisions (PAW, paras.66, 70).

(v) *Industrial democracy* Unions would have extended and new rights to information, consultation and representation (PAW, paras.53–62; *Economic Planning and Industrial Democracy* (1982), EPID; *Social Ownership*, pp.8–9).

27

What impact would these measures have on workers and trade unions? The first two, on health and safety and recognition are rather vague and therefore difficult to evaluate. The proposals that *are* clear – on union facilities, and paid time off for education and training – would primarily benefit workers in less well-organized establishments and those with militant employers who have been unable to secure facilities and time off through collective bargaining.

The redundancy proposals simply require the employer to talk to unions earlier, for longer and more seriously than in the past. But that is all: they do not infringe the employers' right to sack workers as and when he sees fit. The flow of redundants will continue as before except that they will receive slightly more money, and may be offered places on a training programme (see above) whose details are completely unknown.

Industrial action would almost certainly become easier to organize, particularly where secondary action, such as blacking is required. Unions would be largely freed from the iniquitous burden of employer injunctions, and from the astronomical fines and damages inflicted on unions such as the NGA (1982) for their breach of the Employment Acts and subsequent contempt of court. The repeal of these measures would be as popular amongst trade union activists as the repeal in 1974 of the Industrial Relations Act, despite the proposal to re-enact statutory rights that would include the right to a pre-strike ballot. Nevertheless, it is worth entering a note of caution here about the effect of statute law (laws made by Parliament) as compared to judge-made laws (interpretations of statutes and common law). Unions and workers would be granted enhanced rights to organize industrial action and to picket, as well as having some of their traditional immunities restored. Some in the labour movement believe we should now go for a much more extensive set of positive rights, similar to those embodied in the constitutions of most continental countries. Others believe we should simply return to the traditional immunities, in which any trade dispute between workers and employers enjoys protection against damages claims by the strike-bound employers. But the point has been made elsewhere (McCarthy, 1985) that the rights vs immunities debate is a red herring because whatever the language used to frame new laws, the judges will still be called upon to interpret those laws. And over a century of experience shows that they are likely to place a narrow, individualistic anti-union interpretation, however carefully the laws are drafted. This is not an argument against the use of law per se. On the contrary new laws must be enacted, but to be effective they must be policed by strong trade union organization through collective bargaining.

(c) Industrial Democracy

Finally, what of the measures to improve industrial democracy? It is worth discussing these at some length because they occupy such a prominent place in Labour and the TUC's political and economic thinking. It was in 1982 that the Liaison Committee first published in detail proposals in a pamphlet called *Economic Planning and Industrial Democracy*. Its central themes were that unions and their members had a right to be involved in corporate decisions that affected their working lives, and that their involvement through an extension of industrial democracy would constitute the building blocks of a new system of economic planning. Workers and unions would be given new rights to information and to consultation on a wide range of business decisions, and if unions wished they could trigger a process of elections and company reorganization that would give them parity (50-50) board-level representation through worker-directors. Within the framework of a National Economic Plan, top companies would be obliged to draft and submit Agreed Development Plans consistent with government's objectives. These plans would be drawn up with the full involvement of unions and there would be a range of sanctions (price controls, credit restrictions etc.) available for use against companies which produced unacceptable plans or which produced them without union involvement (EPID, 1982; *Partners in Rebuilding Britain*, 1983).

The theme of *agreed* and *negotiated* change is one that comes through strongly in the Committee documents, even in the titles: '*Partners* in Rebuilding Britain' (1983), 'A New *Partnership*, a new Britain' (1986). What is envisaged is a process of joint decision-making based on a consensus about the need for change, about the most appropriate ways of conducting change in enterprises, and about the ways in which costs and benefits are to be shared.

On *paper* these proposals amount to a significant extension of worker and trade union rights, but what is likely to happen in practice? The answer, unfortunately, is not very much and it is important to grasp the reasons for this. Firstly, it is worth recalling that the Bullock Committee reported in 1977 and recommended a statutory right for workers to elect their own directors onto the boards of companies with more than 2000 employees. Worker directors were to constitute a *minority* of the Board, not 50 per cent as some had asked for. Trade union response to Bullock was muted and mixed and both were in evidence at the 1977 TUC Congress debate. Even the mover of the resolution (GMWU) expressed reservations about Bullock's emphasis on worker directors and insisted on the importance of extending collective bargaining as part of a flexible approach to industrial democracy. It was only

29

this flexibility in the resolution which allowed a diverse range of supporters of Bullock (e.g. TGWU) and critics (e.g. EETPU and TASS) to unite behind a single resolution. Ardent supporters of Bullock were thin on the ground. At the following year's Congress, discussion on Labour's White Paper on industrial democracy was perfunctory.

It is true that unions and stewards in a number of companies had become very interested in corporate decision-making and were anxious to extend their rights and their influence in this sphere through workers' alternative Corporate plans; e.g. Lucas Aerospace, GEC, BL, Chrysler, Vickers, Metal Box (Wainwright & Elliot, 1982); Beynon & Wainwright, 1979). Other groups of workers had participated through the Insititute of Workers' Control in discussions about the democratization of particular firms and industrial sectors. There were some notable experiments in creating worker co-operatives. And there were several hundred factory occupations in the 1970s as workers tried to fight redundancies and plant closures. Beyond these major initiatives, workers remained primarily concerned with influencing decisions that affected their immediate job and their workplace, and that influence was based on trade union organization and collective bargaining at local level. But taken overall the interest in formal schemes of company-level industrial democracy was patchy and disappointing.

The result was that the response to Bullock by the trade union movement *as a whole* was feeble and hesitant, a fact that became clear when the CBI counter-attacked. Internal divisions have often prevented the CBI from presenting a united front to government, but faced with the possibility of legally-imposed worker directors the employers were united as never before (Leys, 1985; Elliot, 1983). Their counter attack successfully delayed publication of a White Paper until a few months before the General Election, ensured that its contents were watered down, and exposed uncertainty and vacillation amongst both TUC and Labour leaders.

The charitable interpretation of these events is that unions disliked the Bullock proposals because they were abstract and unconnected to any system of planning, to the existing machinery of collective bargaining and to an expansionary economic policy (Hughes, 1985). There is some truth in the last point, because by 1978 the major concerns of trade unions were focused on jobs (unemployment had reached one million) and wages (living standards had fallen after three years of incomes policy). Nevertheless, the evidence since 1977–78 suggests that union attitudes to industrial democracy are much more deeply ingrained. When *Economic Planning and Industrial Democracy* was placed before the 1982 TUC Congress for discussion, amendment and endorsement, the debate lasted less than ten minutes. Just two delegates spoke from the floor and the issue that bothered them was not industrial democracy *per se*, but whether the proposals were smuggling in an incomes policy 'through the back door' (TUC Congress Report, 1982). Subsequent debates on *Partners in Rebuilding Britain* (1983) and *A New Partnership, A New Britain* (1985) have confirmed the impression of pervasive and overwhelming union disinterest, a state of affairs that is only compounded by the limited research facilities of trade unions compared to the enormous resources that would be needed if the Labour-TUC plans were to come into being (Lane, 1986).

The fact is that for many trade union activists company-level industrial democracy is not currently a major issue, and has not been so for some years. This is clearly a matter of considerable regret for socialists virtually all of whom are committed to some form of workers' control of industry. But it is important that we properly assess contemporary working class consciousness in order to appreciate the most likely responses of people to Labour's new proposals. However, past experience, particularly in the 1960s and 1970s, also suggests that workers' interest in industrial democracy can be heightened under three conditions: firstly, when business decisions directly threaten their livelihoods, as in redundancy situations in the early-middle 1970s; secondly, when workers are confident of taking on the employer, as they were during the strike wave and union membership boom of 1968–74; and thirdly, when government support is available to enhance workers' confidence, as it was during Benn's tenure at the Department of Industry.

On the other side of the class divide, employers' attitudes seemed to have undergone just as little change since the 1970s. When the EEC issued in 1984 two directives on industrial democracy the government, with the full support of the CBI, fought to kill them off. The Vredeling Directive (giving employees the right to elect worker directors onto the boards of large companies) once again provoked a united and militant response from Britain's biggest employers, so much so that it has been shelved until 1991.

This combination of general union disinterest and militant employer opposition would therefore inhibit immediate progress on industrial democracy, and any advances are likely to be patchy and sporadic.

What can we conclude therefore about the significance of the new *collective* rights for workers and trade unions, and their probable impact on party-union relations? Workers and unions would undoubtedly appreciate and benefit from their increased freedom to take industrial action without fear of legal intervention. Unions would also gain new members through whatever recognition machinery was to be enacted, and shop stewards in smaller establishments would benefit from more generous laws on paid time off for educational leave. But all past experience suggests that the *impact* of those

31

gains on workers' attitudes and actions would be minimal. The experience of the Social Contract suggests that enhanced collective rights would not be sufficient to induce union cooperation in pay restraint or in Labour's currently proposed macro-economic policies. And the experiences of Bullock and beyond suggest that most unions would take little advantage of the industrial democracy reforms. As a result their members would be unlikely to derive substantial benefits from them.

(d) Conclusion: Labour's New Social Contract

Let us summarize the argument so far. The next Labour government would almost certainly press for an incomes policy in some form believing it necessary if its efforts to reduce unemployment were not to result in big wage rises and inflation. To secure such a policy it would offer unions a series of individual and collective rights in the context of modest economic expansion, and with some improvements in the welfare state, and would ask for union 'cooperation' over wages. Detailed analysis of these measures suggests they would *not* be sufficient to secure trade union support for wage restraint for the following reasons:

(a) the main beneficiaries of the new rights would be *unorganized workers* who by definition have no voice in trade union policy-making. These groups would derive considerable benefits from Labour's policies at very little cost, if Labour could deliver on its promises.

(b) *trade unions* would gain increased rights and powers particularly in the conduct of industrial action and in the area of industrial democracy. But similar measures in the 1970s did not secure union support for pay restraint and government economic policy for more than a few years either because these measures were only the *minimum* that workers expected (repeal of the Industrial Relations Act) or because they offered rights in which many workers and acivists were not very interested (e.g. industrial democracy).

(c) *organized workers* would therefore achieve some benefits from Labour's proposals but would be asked to bear the brunt of the costs, in the form of wage restraint. How would they be likely to respond? On all past experience they would shoulder these costs for no more than a couple of years and would then rightly insist that their incomes should grow along with everybody else's. Government attempts to thwart their demands would open up a round of confrontations between government and unions, and the 'new Social Contract' would disintegrate.

Since this argument makes some important assumptions about unions and workers it is necessary to elaborate on these points at some length.

4

Economism and Solidarity

(a) Why is Economic Struggle So Important?

Workers who broke through the previous Social Contract in defence of their own immediate sectional economic interests were criticized from a variety of political quarters and on a variety of grounds. Sectional action (or sectionalism) was said to be the bane of the labour movement, and prima facie evidence of a lack of any class outlook. The interests of a particular group of workers were placed by that group above the interests of the working class as a whole. Others objected to the pursuit of purely economic demands, either over wages or over effort levels and job controls, arguing that such militancy was insufficient to challenge capital's rule and that more far-reaching political demands should be fought for. Others again objected to the pursuit of pay differentials by well-organized, male workers in strong bargaining positions and complained of the lack of concern with the low-paid, the unorganized and the unemployed.

Indeed in some quarters it has become quite fashionable to pour scorn on sectional, wages struggles. According to this line of argument workers and unions should take a broader view of the interests of the working class as a whole and should come to recognize there is justice in the demands of the low-paid, unorganized and unemployed to be given priority in the distribution of wealth, even if this means better-paid sections of the working class foregoing improvements in pay they might otherwise have obtained. Wouldn't this form of behaviour, this support for redistribution of incomes *within* the working class, indicate a higher level of class consciousness than the sectional and economic struggles we have seen in the past, and, if my argument is right, will see again in the future?

Let us consider in turn why wages struggle is a central part of trade unionism and what are its consequences for sectionalism and class consciousness. Trade union emphasis on wages is not an expression of a 'crisis of consciousness' (Carter, 1986, p.12) but a product of the material circumstances of most workers and of the particular historical development of class relations in Britain. In 1981 Pond (1983) estimated that 25 per cent of the British workforce were low-paid, i.e. earned less than £85 per week (a figure equal to two-thirds of median adult male earnings). Above these workers, but below the average weekly earnings for the whole economy (£190 per week in 1986) are the majority of manual workers in manufacturing as well as manual and some non-manual employees in the public sector and in private services. Even though these workers are better off than the most lowly-paid, they still experience economic problems as their family income will often fluctuate because of changes in overtime working, shift patterns, bonus pay, part-time hours worked by some members of their family and job insecurity.

Secondly, many workers in Britain, particularly if they belong to trade unions, have come to expect that their standard of living will rise each year, and annual pay bargaining (as opposed to two or three year pay deals) therefore remains deeply rooted in the British system of industrial relations. For the same reason cost of living continues to feature as one of the most salient and widely used arguments in defence of pay rises (Millward & Stevens, 1986, Tables 9.17, 9.18). And so long as there is some level of inflation in the economy, eroding the value of workers' incomes, the pressure for cost of living rises will rightly continue to be very powerful.

Thirdly, standard of living for most people means disposable income or net earnings, and there is no evidence to suggest the 'social wage' – social and other public services – provides adequate compensation for deficiencies in money wages. Social and public services are widely seen as rights paid for through taxes and rates, not a substitute for decent wages.

Fourthly, many workers expect that as their firms become more efficient and increase their sales and profits, then they will share in the proceeds of this economic growth and will rightly insist on the justice and equity of their demands to do so.

Fifthly, many workers will be influenced in their pay demands by the types of pay rise gained by other *similar* groups of workers, or the current levels of pay enjoyed by those groups. Most workers compare themselves with people doing similar jobs, not with the low paid. Skilled engineers do not feel well off just because they earn more than hairdressers, but judge their earnings by comparison with rates paid to engineers in neighbouring firms, and in the light of their employer's ability to pay.

Finally, it should not be thought from any of these points that workers are indifferent to political activity and wider egalitarian objectives. Indeed, the overwhelming success of trade unions in winning their political fund ballots indicates a widespread awareness by workers of the necessity for their unions to have a political voice. But historical evidence suggests that workers will first try to resolve their problems through trade union organization and only when that fails will they turn in large numbers to political action.

Some critics of trade union action argue that it fails to address the special needs of women and black people, rightly pointing out that these groups are poorly represented at leadership levels in most trade unions. But in their defence it should be noted that many unions themselves now acknowledge the problem of under-representation and are seeking, albeit slowly, to do something about it. The TUC has adopted a charter for equality within unions, the proportion of women is rising at most leadership levels, and most of the unions with the largest numbers of female members now make special efforts to promote them within the union. A third or more of the members of the national executives of NUPE, NALGO and the CPSA are women (*Labour Research*, April 1986). Even though the pace of change is slow it still remains the case that in so far as unions succeed in gaining benefits for their members they will be improving the position of women.

The situation with regard to black workers is somewhat similar. Much remains to be done but there is widespread recognition that special efforts must be made to combat racism and to ensure the equal treatment of black workers. Because of the readiness of black workers to join unions, any general improvement in conditions of employment for trade unionists must benefit many black workers, and equal opportunities provisions are becoming far more common in negotiated agreements (Labour Research Department, 1985). Like other workers, women and black people are concerned about pay and conditions and look to unions to advance their interests in these areas. Finally, it is worth noting that struggles between workers and employers, such as the Grunwick strike and the miners' strike can unite workers across lines of gender and race.

Nor should anything said so far be taken to imply that workers lack a social conscience, are indifferent to the poor and the unemployed, and are concerned only for themselves. The point is that even if workers in manufacturing, for instance, *are* concerned about low pay and would genuinely like to contribute to its amelioration, they are faced with a structural problem in doing so. As things stand presently, the immediate beneficiary of wage restraint by manufacturing workers would be their employers and their profits. A socially conscious and rational worker would not support pay restraint in the interests of the low paid unless he/she could see some mechanism for translating their restraint to the benefit of low paid workers without undue cost to themselves. In other words the problem with moral appeals to workers to restrain their sectional pay demands is not that they fall on deaf ears, but that no channels currently exist for the translation of one person's restraint into another worker's benefit. Whether and how such channels could be created is a question I consider shortly.

For all these reasons – the material circumstances and customary expectations of workers, the institution of annual pay bargaining, and the demand for a share in the benefits of economic growth – unions will continue to place pay demands at the top of their bargaining agenda, and rightly so. The idea that pay can be pushed off its pre-eminent position in trade union thinking and action is an illusion.

(b) Does Economic Struggle Develop Political Consciousness?

But a second line of attack on wages struggle makes a different point, and claims that its effects on political class consciousness are minimal. This is the familiar Leninist critique of trade union action. What can we say about this argument? Firstly, whatever its limitations the wages issue has mobilized more workers in struggle in Britain than any other trade union demand. The history of strikes as far back as statistics go (1888) shows that the periods of widespread industrial conflict, with high strike frequency and large numbers of strikers, were also the periods when the greatest proportion of strikes was fought over wages. In other words the high-water marks of working class mobilization in industrial conflict were *also* periods when industrial action was dominated by the wages issue: 1916–22, 1968–74, 1978–79 (Cronin, 1979, Table B3). In between these 'strike waves' the proportion of strikes over wages tended to be lower.

Secondly, the strike waves of 1916–22, 1968–74, and 1978–79 have been associated with quite different implications for class consciousness. 1916–22 was a period of worldwide industrial and political militancy which in Britain witnessed the creation of a militant shop stewards' movement with a strong revolutionary presence in its leadership, the formation of the Communist Party, a substantial rise in the working class vote for the Labour Party in place of the Liberals, and a centralization of power in the TUC in preparation for the struggles to come. 1968–74 showed much weaker and more contradictory effects: one Labour government was defeated, but two more were elected, unions deployed industrial action for political ends against the Industrial Relations Act, a wave of factory occupations swept the country affecting over 500 workplaces, trade union membership grew rapidly and shop steward organization began to develop in new areas of trade unionism in the public sector. The Labour Party and the TUC both swung leftwards in their economic and industrial policy (a somewhat shallow move in the case of the Labour Party as events were to show), the far left grew and established a few footholds in the organized working class though the decline of Communist Party membership continued. 1978–79 needs little description as the divisions and recriminations of the period are sufficiently well known: Labour lost the election to a particularly virulent and reactionary Tory Party and trade union popularity plunged in the opinion polls despite a continued growth in its membership.

What can we conclude from this sketchy overview of three periods of wages militancy about its implications for class consciousness? If we regard party voting, party membership, forms of organization and struggle, union and party policy, and popular attitudes as valid (if crude) measures of class consciousness then we are forced to this conclusion: the wages struggle in and of itself has no pre-determined effects on class consciousness. Its effects will vary between different periods and conjunctures: at some periods it will mobilize and radicalize large numbers, at other periods its effects will be minimal. It is the *context* of wages struggle, above all the activities, organization and influence of political forces that shape the outcomes of economic struggles. To write off such struggles as inherently limited is an error in one direction. Equally to see in every isolated wage struggle the germs of political class consciousness is an error in the opposite direction. Socialists should therefore support wages struggles as the core activity of trade unions, and as a principal means of developing class consciousness in certain conditions.

One final criticism of economic struggle needs to be considered briefly, and that is its sectional character. According to this view trade union action is often taken by sections of workers in pursuit of their own particular interests. At best it is said to bring benefit to weaker groups of employees such as women, and at worst it may do considerable damage to other trade unionists and to the public, as in the 'winter of discontent'. It is undoubtedly true that the bulk of trade union activity is concerned with local issues affecting particular groups of workers and in that sense is sectional. But since workers join trades unions for protection, and for improvements at their place of work, this type of sectional action is inevitable so long as unions remain democratic. But what about strikes that damage the public, or the consumers of services? Strikes by teachers, social workers, nurses and other service workers? Or what about sectional strikes by skilled workers in defence of their differentials?

In these situations workers have frequently been faced with a particularly difficult dilemma: either they could support a general, labour movement policy, such as the Social Contract in the interests of unity even though they were suffering cuts in living standards, *or* they could take industrial action, knowing that this would bring them into conflict with the rest of the movement. Whilst the principle of trade union unity will be endorsed by most trade unionists, it cannot be expected to operate in the absence of consensus, and where large sections of the movement (such as low paid manual workers in 1978–79) are being clearly disadvantaged. The 'winter of discontent' *was*, in one aspect, an expression of sectional and economistic militancy; but it was also a revolt by workers against an unjust incomes policy and against Labour's economic mismanagement, and *both* aspects must be appreciated. Sectional action will therefore remain as a normal and common feature of trade union action.

5

Alternative Policies

Given this is the case, two major questions remain. Precisely how and under what conditions will trade union struggles and demands develop class consciousness amongst workers and assist in the expansion of their rights and powers? And what can socialists do to help create and exploit these conditions to maximum advantage? At the risk of some oversimplification there are two broad strategies that are worth considering. In the first case trade unions engage in some form of partnership with a Labour government on terms considerably more radical than anything seen in the past and as part of a coordinated strategy to shift the balance of wealth and power away from capital and towards labour. The second strategy assumes that such an arrangement will prove either impossible or short-lived, and Labour's economic and industrial policies can instead be shifted in a more radical direction through the impact of industrial militancy. Let us therefore consider each strategy in turn.

(a) A Radical Union-Government Partnership

Trade Union Demands

If Labour is to win a majority at the next election it must begin the task now of developing a coherent alternative, capable of attracting majority support from working people and their families. The Conservative Government's economic record, its proposed new attacks on trade union rights as outlined in the paper 'Trade Unions and their Members', its proposed introduction of a highly regressive poll tax and its indifference towards large regions of the country, are likely to provoke widespread resistance. There will certainly be scope for the Labour Party and the trade unions to work together to lead this resistance and defeat Government plans. But such resistance will be stronger if Labour has positive alternatives to offer. In some cases this will require a modification of existing plans and perspectives, but it will also require a greater preparedness to confront capitalist power in Britain, above all in the City.

In this context how should trade unions respond to Labour proposals for an incomes policy and what demands should they be making on the Labour Party and on a future Labour government?

Firstly, for the reasons outlined earlier in Chapter 5, wage demands will continue to figure prominently on union bargaining agenda and workers will continue to expect real increases in their wages as judged by the cost of living. The most that trade unions could possibly hope to agree with a Labour government would therefore be a *slower rate of real wage increase* than might otherwise occur under a regime of 'free collective bargaining'. A wage standstill or a wage cut would not have the slightest chance of being accepted.

Secondly, in order to maintain such a policy it would be essential for *price controls* to be introduced on a wide range of consumer goods. Otherwise a rise in the rate of inflation would simply lead union negotiators to submit bigger wage demands in order to maintain and improve their members' living standards. Even during the years of recession unions have used a rise in the cost of living as the major justification for their annual pay rises, and they would certainly continue to do so under a future Labour government. We know from past experience that effective price controls are extremely difficult to operate and that employers will try to devise countless ways of getting round them. But a policy of price controls would at least establish a climate of opinion that was hostile to unwarranted price rises and this might have a deterrent effect on firms.

Thirdly, it would be necessary to meet the objection raised earlier to pay restraint, which was that no mechanism exists for channelling the results of one worker's restraint into benefits for other workers instead of high profits for the employer. There would have to be strict *controls on rates of profit and steep taxes* on 'excess profits' that were earmarked for agreed social expenditures, despite all the difficulties of measuring and therefore controlling profits. Otherwise, as argued earlier, there will be no incentive for

41

a socially-conscious rational worker to exercise any kind of restraint on his/her own pay demands.

Fourthly, in view of the continuing high levels of unemployment, and the continuing flow of redundancies, Labour would have to implement much *tougher measures against redundancy* than those proposed in *People at Work* and discussed earlier. A combination of measures would need to be set in place to ensure that redundancies were kept to an absolute minimum, and job protection guaranteed as far as possible especially in areas of high unemployment. These might include compulsory redeployment of labour by employers, directed investment into regions of high unemployment and job loss, and guaranteed reimbursement of retraining, relocation, rehousing and other costs associated with labour market mobility so that redundant workers bore as few costs as possible.

These measures would deal with the primary concerns of most workers, namely their level of pay and their job security. But it would also be necessary to ensure advances on the wider issue of *industrial democracy*. Labour's proposed rights in this area – to information, consultation and representation – have yet to be fully tested in more than a handful of British companies. But what little experience we do have underlines the immense difficulties in the path of industrial democracy. Studies of the Post Office (Batstone et al. 1983) and British Steel (Brannen et al. 1976) revealed numerous ways in which large and powerful corporations could circumvent or neutralize trade union influence. Achieving real influence over decisions will be even harder in the private sector multinational corporations, such as Lucas, GEC or Ford whose global scale of operations provides them with a permanent power advantage over organized labour. Only a combination of trade union and State pressure will force many of these large multinationals to negotiate seriously with unions, and that will require that a Labour government is willing to use a wide range of sanctions as well as incentives to force such firms to behave reasonably. A refusal to do this would leave many unions in a weak bargaining position, and turn their experience of 'industrial democracy' into frustration and bitterness.

At the very minimum therefore trade unions should insist on a labour movement policy embracing a slow, but real growth of wages, tough controls on prices, controls and steep taxes on 'excess profits', tougher measures of job protection and avoidance of redundancy, and tougher measures to ensure that those workers striving for 'industrial democracy' can exert real influence over their employers' decisions.

What additional measures should trade unions urge on a Labour government, over and above these minima? In the field of *collective rights*, discussed earlier, the rights to strike and to picket must be given the widest possible protection. Whether this is achieved through the restoration of trade union immunities or the creation of new rights is a matter for debate. It must also be made easier for trade unions to recruit workers and to obtain recognition for collective bargaining purposes, though whether this should be done through coordinated union action, through machinery of contract compliance and/or through new legal rights is still a matter for discussion (cf. McCarthy, 1985, p.31; Mortimer, 1986). Thirdly, unions should be free to conduct solidarity actions with fellow workers as they see fit, unhindered by legal restrictions on 'secondary action'. Fourthly, trade unions should be able to spend their funds on any matter that is covered in the objectives laid down in their rule books. The distinction between 'general' and 'political' funds should therefore be recognized as an infringement of trade union control over their own finances and should be abolished. Political activity, broadly defined, is an integral part of trade unionism and should be financed out of general income, and not out of separate funds, subject to special rules and procedures, forced on the trade union movement in 1913, again in 1984 and most recently in the Government Green Paper (HMSO, 1987). Finally, trade unions should be left to decide for themselves how to consult their members over strike action, and how to elect or appoint their executives and officials.

In the field of *economic policy*, unions should go beyond Labour's proposed improvements in training and education, and insist that all adults of working age be provided with a statutory right to work, education or training. Clearly this would take some time to translate into effective guarantees but the passage of such a measure would signal both Labour's commitment to a wholesale attack on unemployment, and its determination to see through such a policy. Trade unions should also seek government assistance in further reducing working hours, in the first instance by setting an example with their own workforce. The 35 hour week should become an interim target, with the 32 hour week being the longer-term aim. Radical reductions of this scale would have some impact on the level of unemployment, but they would be valued by many workers for creating more leisure time.

In the field of social policy, trade unions should be insisting both on substantial increases in welfare and social service expenditures in order to reduce the problem of poverty and greatly expanded facilities for childcare, as well as the restoration of steeply progressive taxation. The salaries bonanza in the City of London has seen people earning tens, even hundreds of thousands of pounds, for organizing speculation on the Stock Exchange. There is every reason to believe that heavy taxation of such inflated incomes would be immmensely popular, and would signal Labour's determination to drastically curb the 'conspicuous consumption' of the rich. In addition a Labour government would also need to take appropriate measures to deal with resistance to all these policies from the City and elsewhere, and examples of measures such as exchange controls are described in Glyn (1985).

The successful pursuit of this whole package of measures, coupled with a strong trade union campaign behind them could help shift the balance of wealth and power in Britain, and stimulate class consciousness, and trade union organization and political activity amongst workers.

The Prospects of Success

What are the prospects of such a strategy? Much depends on the willingness of a Labour government to carry out its side of such a partnership and the willingness of unions and their members to trust the government. It also depends on the capacity of trade unions to act in concert, taking a broad view of the interests of the movement as a whole.

Overseas experience, particularly from Sweden provides one possible model for this type of labour movement strategy and is therefore worth looking at more closely. Organizing over 80 per cent of the workforce, the Swedish trade unions wield considerable power, and since the big strikes of the 1930s have worked very closely with the Social Democratic Party. From the early 1970s the main federation, the LO, has pioneered a series of major policy initiatives, in industrial democracy, health and safety, and most recently the idea of wage-earner funds. The basic proposal is that company profits in excess of a specified limit are paid into a fund which will, over a period of between 10 and 30 years eventually become the biggest and most powerful source of Swedish investment capital. Unions will then be in a position to direct and control the business strategies of the major Swedish corporations in conjunction with their partners. In practice the scale of the proposal has since been reduced, but the basic measures have now been enacted. In addition the unions have pressed over the years for continued improvements in welfare spending and enhanced public expenditure to maintain full employment, with the result that the Swedish ratio of public expenditure to GDP is amongst the highest in the capitalist world (Therborn 1984).

In return, unions have underutilized their market bargaining power and have not pushed up wages as fast as they might have done. They have also sought to minimize the incidence of strikes, and they have, for the most part, cooperated in technical change on the grounds that a high productivity economy is a precondition for a high wage economy. Furthermore, government commitment to full employment helps ensure that workers bear only a fraction of the costs of technical change and are provided with retraining, rehousing and other allowances to help them over transition periods between jobs and occupations (Cameron, 1984).

Some socialists would oppose in principle any agreement between a trade union movement and a government that restrained the rate of growth of real wages under capitalism. Only under socialism, they would say, should such agreements be entertained. My own position is that whether unions push hardest on the wages front, on the working week, on equal opportunities or whatever, and whether they should ease up on one demand in order to press home another, are tactical and strategic questions for unions and their members to decide.

So what are the prospects for such a radical partnership in Britain? If we compare Britain and Sweden we are forced to the conclusion that as matters stand currently the prospects are bleak. To begin with the Swedish labour movement is more powerful than its British counterpart, organizing 85 per cent of the workforce compared to Britain's 51 per cent. Secondly, the central union federations in Sweden, the LO and the TCO, enjoy considerably more power over their affiliate members than the British TUC. The Swedish federations engage in industry and multi-industry bargaining with employers and government, unlike the TUC, and have far greater powers of intervention in the affairs of their affiliates. For those two reasons – union density, and centralization of power – Swedish labour is capable of acting in a much more disciplined and united way than the TUC and its affiliates.

Thirdly, the Swedish Social Democrats (sometimes in conjunction with the Swedish Communist Party) have proved far more willing than the British Labour Party to pursue radical measures when in office, and to consolidate support for such policies through mass membership education (Linton, 1985).

Fourth, employers in Sweden have lived under Social Democratic governments for 45 out of the last 51 years and have therefore had to come to terms with the Left in a way that British employers have not. Faced with a government measure they disliked, Swedish employers have had to reckon *without* the possibility of electoral defeat for the Left. British employers on the other hand have been more willing to put up stiff resistance to measures such as Bullock's industrial democracy proposals confident in the belief that Labour would soon be out of office and the measures would be scrapped by the incoming Tory administration. Fifth, Sweden's employers are well organized in a powerful and highly centralized federation, the SAF, whose membership and bargaining role enables it to discipline its *own* members and ensure they stick to collective agreements. The degree of centralization and discipline in the organizations of *both* labour and capital has made each side

45

more willing to enter into high-level tripartite negotiations and agreements confident in the belief that the other side will deliver. In Britain by contrast, the degree of decentralization both in the TUC and the CBI provides no grounds for anyone – government, TUC, CBI – being confident in the ability of the others to deliver their members' support.

Finally, Swedish capital is highly concentrated, heavily orientated to world markets because of the tiny domestic market, and predominately national rather than multinational (Ingham, 1974). Its considerable involvement in world markets (compared to British capital) means that Swedish capital is under intense pressure to remain competitive, a fact that is recognized and accepted by the main trade union federation, the LO. Historically, employers have sought to promote productivity growth through a strategy of cooperation, both because of labour's capacity to damage their interests and because of labour's willingness to cooperate. The national character of Swedish capital has meant that the opportunity to 'exit' overseas, rather than confront organized labour, has not been so readily available, as for say British or American capital. As a result of these factors Swedish capital has had powerful incentives to cooperate with labour. In Hirschman's terms the incentive to practice 'loyalty' has outweighed the advantages of 'voice' and the limited possibilities of 'exit'.

It is this pattern of incentives, itself a product of Sweden's historical development, its economic structure and the organizational forms of labour and capital, that helps us understand and appreciate the viability of the Swedish labour movement's strategy, and by the same token helps us realize why the conditions for its pursuit are largely absent from Britain (Kelly, in press).

b) Industrial Militancy and its Political Consequences

The more plausible scenario is that Labour would attempt to operate a Social Contract but would be seen by trade unionists not to be delivering its side of the deal. The contract would run for a couple of years and then break down as Labour's policies failed to satisfy people's expectations. On past experience even the merest hint of radical policies would frighten the City and sections of big business, and numerous forms of economic sabotage, intended or not, would be set in motion. If Labour refused to confront these problems, but turned instead on its own supporters, appealing for further restraint and austerity, rapid disillusion amongst workers would be the result.

The situation would be even more tense if we consider the prospect of a

Labour-Alliance pact, or a Labour government accommodating to Alliance pressure. The Alliance has consistently sided with the Conservatives in their programme of anti-union legislation. They accused the Government's most recent Green Paper, *Trade Unions and Their Members*, of stealing the Alliance's own policies and they are even more firmly committed to compulsory secret ballots than the current Labour leadership. On the economic and industrial front their commitment to mild reflation has always co-existed with a deliberate refusal to institute the kinds of controls over production, investment and trade that would form the cornerstones of Left economic strategy. The Alliance's policies for beating unemployment are remarkably similar both in their means and their ambition to those of the Labour Party, sharing an emphasis on selected infra-structural investment and special employment measures (see proposals by one of their leading economists, Layard, 1986). Finally, the Alliance has been quite explicit about the necessity for an incomes policy (cf. Layard, 1986; SDP, Liberal Alliance, 1983). If Labour's leaders allow themselves to be drawn into any understanding or agreement with the Alliance – even if this is tacit rather than open – then this could only accentuate the right wing elements in Labour's policy and create conditions for a damaging breach with its trade union supporters.

So what exactly would be the issues and arenas of conflict between a right wing Labour government and the unions?

There are several possible 'flashpoints', the first involving organized private sector workers in manufacturing. Assume that Labour's reflation increased demand in the economy and continued the increase in manufacturing output and profits that began in 1983. If we also assume a reduction in unemployment (down by a million in two years is the official target) and a modest growth in trade union membership, then union negotiators would be more confident in pushing for larger wage settlements. In order to protect profits these increased costs would be passed on in higher prices (unless they were absorbed by higher productivity). Negotiators would respond the following year with larger claims so that a wage-price spiral began. At this point the Government would become concerned at the impact of private sector wage rises on public sector pay and spending. Broadly speaking, Labour is committed to some form of pay comparability between the public and the private sectors, and a faster movement in private sector settlements and earnings would soon feed through into public sector negotiations. The more rapidly private sector earnings rose the more incentive Labour would have to avoid similar rises in the public sector. This is because the public sector is very labour intensive so that a rise in labour costs would have a dramatic effect on total public spending and therefore on government borrowing (PSBR).

Government would then be faced with a dilemma: either it could try to restrain public sector pay whilst private sector pay rose more rapidly, which is a sure recipe for a wave of public sector strikes. Or alternatively it could try to restrain earnings growth in the private sector which past experience suggests is exceptionally difficult and politically damaging, unless some very radical measures are offered to trade unions as a quid pro quo, and that seems unlikely.

Another flashpoint could arise over public sector pay and employment. Increased expenditure in the public sector services would be intended to create more jobs and reduce unemployment. The labour-intensive character of many of these services means that the total cost per job created is considerably lower than in manufacturing industry (it is also lower because public sector service wages are generally less than in manufacturing). However, unions in these sectors have taken many years of comparatively low pay settlements, and many of them (such as civil servants) have very limited opportunities to boost their earnings through shift work, overtime or bonuses. The pattern of large, long and bitter public sector strikes since 1979 indicates a reservoir of discontent over pay, but also over working conditions (in the civil service, for instance) and job losses. It is reasonable to assume that whilst many negotiators will welcome a statutory national minimum wage, as it will clearly benefit some of their members, they are also likely to regard it as just that: a *minimum* to be built on through collective bargaining. This attitude will be encouraged by the low level at which the minimum is likely to be set (£80 per week) and by the TUC's own belief that the attack on low pay must proceed through legislation *and* collective bargaining. There will therefore be immense pressure in the public sector to recover ground lost in the years of recession when compared with the private sector, leading to the real possibility of a wages explosion that would consume additional public spending in the form of higher earnings for those in work rather than jobs for those out of work. Appeals to exercise restraint *are* likely to fall on deaf ears amongst public sector manual workers, many of whom are involuntary and long-serving members of the army of the low paid.

The third possible flashpoint for government-union conflict could come over redundancies. Despite the shake out of 25 per cent of the manufacturing workforce, industry is still shedding labour. In the year to September 1986 the total workforce in manufacturing was cut by 110,000, and there are large-scale redundancies still to come. The heroic struggle by the miners (1984–85) showed the potential for mobilization against a large-scale programme of redundancies in a major public corporation with a well-organized workforce and a militant union leadership. And the continued shedding of jobs in the mining industry does not preclude further struggles for the defence of jobs and conditions. British Telecom still plans a substantial cut in its workforce because of higher productivity brought about through its System X exchanges. The Post Office has had plans in hand for several years to reorganize and streamline the postal workforce. And British Rail has so far made only small inroads into cutting its workforce despite long-standing plans to do so.

Significantly the four major unions in communications, post and railways, the NCU, UCW, NUR and ASLEF, have recently lost a much smaller percentage of their membership than many other trade unions. UCW membership for instance at 202,000 in 1980 and by 1985 still stood at over 195,000, a fall of under 4 per cent. Insofar as Labour is anxious to modernize industry and improve its efficiency, and this is a constant theme in Liaison Committee documents, then big job losses could come about in public corporations which still have powerful and well organized unions with almost 100 per cent membership density. Indeed the 1987 telecommunications strike showed the strength of feeling and determination of the telephone engineers to resist productivity improvements that would cut jobs. In a climate of rising expectations under a Labour government and with more legal protection for industrial action workers may feel more confident about taking on their employers in major battles over job losses, redundancy and redeployment. It was in struggles over such issues in the 1970s that a minority of workers developed a strong interest in 'industrial democracy' and workers' control of corporate decision-making.

In other words, if Labour took the British economy further out of recession, and continued the restoration of profitability, coupled with a fall in unemployment, it would also help to raise people's expectations about their living standards. This in turn would create more confidence among trade unionists, and if their bargaining demands encountered serious resistance from employers, then the result could be a growth of industrial unrest. Past experience shows that strike frequency rose dramatically at the end of the Great Depression (1889–94), and at the end of the inter-war Depression (1935–46), as well as at the end of the Edwardian boom (1910–14, 1915–22), and at the end of the post-war boom (1968–74, 1978–79).

Such periods of industrial militancy create both problems as well as opportunities for socialists, particularly under a Labour government. The traditional response of the Labour Right to a rising tide of worker militancy has in the past, and will in the future, be to call for order and restraint on the grounds that strikes will only damage the popularity of trade unions and the government and prepare the way for electoral defeat. And this indeed was the pattern of events in 1968-70 under Harold Wilson, and in 1978-79 under James Callaghan. More recently we have seen strikes and demonstrations across Europe as workers protested against the austerity measures of mostly socialist governments. Craxi in Italy, Gonzalez in Spain, Papandreou in Greece and Chirac in France: all these leaders have precipitated waves of industrial unrest, particularly by Communist-led unions trying to defend workers' living standards and jobs.

But the consequences of accepting 'order and restraint' could be dire. The Labour governments of the past have always come under strong pressure from the City and big business to moderate their industrial and economic policies, and swing to the Right. The governments of Wilson and Callaghan went along this road and then faced the task of quelling the inevitable discontent among trade unionists, and appealing for restraint and 'patience' in order to keep Labour in office. But past experience shows that to acquiesce in this process is to strengthen the very forces in the City and big business whose interests it is designed to serve.

How then should socialists respond to a wave of industrial militancy under a Labour government? Firstly, the mobilization of workers in struggle should be encouraged because it is a necessary (though not a sufficient) condition for the development of trade union organization, and the improvement of workers' living standards, and because it can help to stimulate class consciousness. Mobilization can help to encourage the growth of shop steward organization and of trade union membership, as in 1968-74, and 1978-79. In other words trade union struggle can help to develop one of Labour's primary resources, union membership and organization. And if workers are securing a growing number of victories through struggle this will help to build confidence, and a sense of their own power. This power is something that a Labour government should aim to build on in pursuit of the objectives of the labour movement as a whole.

Secondly, working class resistance to wage restraint or to job losses can provide a major source of pressure on a Labour government, and act as a counter-vailing force against the influence of capital. A Labour government that believes it can ask for major sacrifices from its own supporters will have little incentive to challenge and resist the pressures of business that make such sacrifices necessary in the first place. But a government faced with resistance from workers could be another matter. Under such conditions the Labour Left would be in a much stronger position to challenge the economic, industrial and other policies of the Labour Right which had brought it into open conflict with its trade union base.

Thirdly, the effective mobilization of trade union and left-wing Labour pressure for more radical policies will require considerable membership organization within and between unions. Rank-and-file and broad Left organization has been well developed in quite a number of unions over the years, though there has been some decline during the 1980s. A number of unions have developed different types of militant and left-wing organization, and some have a tradition of strong, left-wing leadership.

Fourthly, the Labour Left, trade unions and other social forces would then be in a stronger position to insist on the adoption of more radical economic and industrial policies, and to open negotiations with the dominant forces in the government on the terms of a new, radical partnership of the type described earlier.

Such a partnership, and the radical policies it would entail, will be difficult to negotiate and even harder to implement. British trade unions do not have a powerful, centralized federation like their Swedish counterparts. The decentralized system of bargaining makes it extraordinarily difficult to pursue any general bargaining strategy. Employers are not used to extensive tripartite discussions which pose serious threats to their prerogatives and profits. For these, and the other reasons given earlier, any radical union-government partnership in Britain would be extremely precarious, subject to sectional disaffection from Labour's own ranks, and outright hostility and sabotage from capital, not to mention the State apparatus.

If the risks of such a strategy are high, so too are the potential benefits. The alternative however would be another right-wing Labour government headed for electoral defeat, and the return of the Conservatives or the Alliance. The Left's aim is therefore not just to secure the election of a Labour government, but to obtain a series of re-elections based on radical economic, industrial and social policies that will bring about 'an irreversible shift of wealth and power to working people and their families', and to the unemployed and the poor who have borne the brunt of British capitalism in crisis.

In or out of government, Labour's relations with its trade union supporters will be the key to its ability to tackle the reactionary forces in Britain and create a more just and equal society. To regard the trade unions simply as a source of funds and to ignore the basic objectives of trade unionism would be shortsighted and counter-productive. Labour should, in future, pay far more attention to mobilizing its impressive political support within the unions, using it as a vital ally in bringing about radical changes within society as a whole – the ending of mass unemployment, the regeneration of a productive economy, the rehabilitation of welfare and education, and the progressive dismantling of all the structures of a class divided social order.

51

6

Summary

This pamphlet has argued that:

(1) The logic of Labour's current proposed economic policies would require it to adopt some form of incomes policy, and therefore to 'sell' such a policy to trade unions as part of a new Social Contract.

(2) Labour would enact a series of individual and collective legal rights that would bring considerable benefits to unorganized and low paid workers, some benefits and freedoms for trade unions as organizations, but few benefits to organized workers in manufacturing and parts of the public sector. Organized workers however would be asked to bear many of the costs of Labour's programme, especially in the form of continued wage restraint, and will be loath to do so.

(3) Many workers would be unwilling to tolerate wage restraint because of the centrality of wages for trade unions and their members and because of their experiences of Labour in office during the Social Contract of 1974–79.

(4) Furthermore many workers still retain considerable bargaining power because trade union organization, membership and finances have survived the recession remarkably well, despite all the talk of labour movement crisis. The durability of trade unionism places workers in a relatively good position to influence the policies of a future Labour government and push them in a radical direction.

(5) There are two main routes through which this influence could be secured: one is through a form of partnership between the unions and a Labour government around radical economic, industrial and social policies. The other is through the pressure of industrial militancy. These routes need not be mutually exclusive but their emphases and implications are different.

(6) In order to secure some form of partnership with a Labour government, unions should press for a series of radical economic, industrial and social policies over and above those currently on offer in conjunction with a slower rate of growth of real wages (*not* wage reductions or a wage standstill).

(7) Unions should call for the full restoration of their rights to strike, picket and secure recognition, with appropriate modifications to protect them against judicial interference; the separation between general union funds and political funds should be abolished and unions allowed to spend money according to the wishes of their members; there should be a statutory right to work, education or training; working hours should be progressively and radically reduced; welfare spending should be increased and steep taxes restored for the rich.

(8) The very least that unions should accept from a Labour government are tough price controls, taxes on 'excess' profits above an agreed level, measures to protect jobs and avoid redundancies and tougher sanctions on firms who refused to cooperate in schemes of 'industrial democracy'.

(9) If a Labour government did not adopt these measures, but still tried to persist with some form of incomes policy, then it would generate considerable discontent amongst organized workers that would express itself in the form of industrial militancy.

(10) In these circumstances, socialists should use the pressure of working class discontent to try to push Labour's policies leftward, along the lines described above, and should actively oppose accommodation with the Alliance.

(11) If Labour is unable to form a government then it should use its resources to campaign for the defence of trade union rights and workers' living standards, and for socialist policies designed to bring about 'an irreversible shift of wealth and power in favour of working people and their families'.

References

ACAS (1986) *Annual Report 1985*. London, Advisory, Conciliation and Arbitration Service.

Atkinson, J. and Gregory, D. (1986) 'A Flexible Future: Britain's Dual Labour Force', *Marxism Today*, April.

Bain, G. and Price, R. (1983) 'Union Growth' in Bain, G., (ed.) *Industrial Relations in Britain*. Oxford, Blackwell.

Batstone, E. (1984) *Working Order*. Oxford, Blackwell.

Batstone, E. et al. (1983) *Unions on the Board*. Oxford, Blackwell.

Beynon, H. and Wainwright, H. (1979) *The Workers' Report on Vickers*. London, Pluto Press.

Brannen, P. et al. (1976) *The Worker Directors*. London, Hutchinson.

Cameron, D. R. (1984) 'Social Democracy, Corporatism, Labour Quiescence and the Representation of Economic Interest in Advanced Capitalist Society' in Goldthorpe, J. H. (ed.) *Order and Conflict in Contemporary Capitalism*. Oxford, Clarendon Press.

Carter, P. (1986) *Trade Unions: the New Reality. The Communist View*. London, Communist Party of Great Britain.

Coates, K. and Topham, T. (1986) *Trade Unions and Politics*. Oxford, Blackwell.

Cronin, J. E. (1979) *Industrial Conflict in Modern Britain*. London, Croom Helm.

Department of Employment *Department of Employment Gazette* (various issues).

Dickens, L. et al. (1985) *Dismissed*. Oxford, Blackwell.

Elliot, J. (1978) *Conflict or Cooperation: the Growth of Industrial Democracy*. London, Kogan Page.

Fogarty, M. (1986) *Trade Unions and British Industrial Development*. London, Policy Studies Institute.

Fox, A. (1985) *History and Heritage: the Social Origins of the British Industrial Relations System*. London, Allen & Unwin.

Glyn, A. (1985) *A Million Jobs a Year*. London, Verso.

Glyn, A. and Harrison, J. (1980) *The British Economic Disaster*. London, Pluto Press.

Goodhart, G. (1985) 'Prices, Incomes and Consumer Issues' in Jowell, R. and Witherspoon, S. *British Social Attitudes: the 1985 Report*. Aldershot, Gower.

Gregory, M. et al. (1985) 'Pay Settlements in Manufacturing 1979–84: Evidence from the CBI Databank', *British Journal of Industrial Relations*, 23(3), November.

Hain, P. (1986) *Political Strikes*. London, Viking.

HMSO (1987) *Trade Unions and Their Members*. London, HMSO.

Hobsbawm, E. (1985) 'Retreat into Extremism', *Marxism Today*, April.

Hughes, J. (1986) 'Industrial Democracy and Socialist Priorities' in Coates, K. (ed.) *Freedom and Fairness: Empowering People at Work*. Nottingham, Spokesman.

Ingham, G. (1974) *Strikes and Industrial Conflict*. London, Macmillan.

Kellner, P. (1987) 'Two Nations Born from One Vote' *The Independent*, 13 June.

Kelly, J. (forthcoming publication) *Agents of Socialism or Partners in Capitalism? Marxism and trade unions*. London, Lawrence & Wishart.

Kinnock, N. (1986) *Making Our Way*. Oxford, Blackwell.

Lane, T. (1986) 'Economic Democracy: are the Trade Unions Equipped?'. *Industrial Relations Journal*, 17(4).

Labour Party (1986) 'Social Ownership', Statement by the National Executive Committee to 1986 Conference.

Labour Research Department (1985) *Black Workers, Trade Unions and the Law*. London, LRD.

Labour Research Department (1986) *Part-Time Workers*. London, LRD.

Labour Research Department (1986) 'Union Political Funds', *Labour Research*. London, LRD.

Labour Research Department (1986) 'Women in the Unions', *Labour Research*. London, LRD.

Layard, R. (1986) *How To Beat Unemployment*. Oxford, Oxford University Press.

Leys, C. (1985) 'Thatcherism and British Manufacturing: a Question of Hegemony'. *New Left Review*, 151, May–June.

Linton, M. (1985) *The Swedish Road to Socialism*. London, Fabian Tract 503.

McCarthy, W. (1985) *Freedom at Work: Towards the Reform of Tory Employment Laws*. London, Fabian Tract 508.

Martin, J. and Roberts, C. (1985) *Women and Employment*. London, DE/OPCS.

Millward, N. and Stevens, M. (1986) *British Workplace Industrial Relations 1980–1984*. Aldershot, Gower.

Mortimer, J. (1986) 'Let Trade Unions Do their Job!' in Coates, K. (ed.) *Freedom and Fairness*. Nottingham, Spokesman.

Pond, C. (1983) 'Wages Councils, the Unorganised and the Low Paid' in Bain, G. (ed.) *Industrial Relations in Britain*. Oxford, Blackwell.

Pond, C. and Winyard, S. (1983) *The Case For a National Minimum Wage*. London, Low Pay Unit.

Prest, A. R. and Coppock, D. J. (1982) *The UK Economy 9th Edition*. London, Weidenfeld & Nicholson.

Rowthorn, B. and Grahl, J. (1986) 'Dodging the Taxing Questions', *Marxism Today*, November.

SDP-Liberal Alliance (1983) *Working Together for Britain*. London, SDP-Liberal Alliance.

Sherman, B. (1986) *The State of the Unions*. Chichester, Wiley.

Therborn, G. (1984) 'The Prospects of Labour and the Transformation of Advanced Capitalism'. *New Left Review*, 145, May–June.

TUC *Congress Reports* (various years).

TUC (1973) *Economic Policy and the Cost of Living*. London, TUC.

TUC (1986) *Economic Review 1986*. London, TUC.

TUC-Labour Party Liaison Committee (1982) *Economic Planning and Industrial Democracy*. London, TUC.

TUC-Labour Party Liaison Committee (1983) *Partners in Rebuilding Britain*. London, TUC.

TUC-Labour Party Liaison Committee (1985) *A New Partnership, A New Britain*. London, TUC.

TUC-Labour Party Liaison Committee (1986a) *People at Work: New Rights, New Responsibilities*. London, TUC.

TUC-Labour Party Liaison Committee (1986b) *Low Pay: Policies and Priorities*. London, TUC.

TUC-Labour Party Liaison Committee (1987) *Work to Win*. London, TUC.

Undy, R. and Martin, R. (1984) *Ballots and Trade Union Democracy*. Oxford, Blackwell.

Wainwright, H. and Elliot, D. (1982) *The Lucas Plan*. London, Allison & Busby.

Wilson, A. (1986) 'The Debate over Labour Law: New Rights or New Responsibilities' in Coates, K. (ed.) *Freedom and Fairness*. Nottingham, Spokesman.

Printed and bound by CPI Group (UK) Ltd, Croydon, CR0 4YY

22/04/2026

02095406-0014